TEACHER
LEADER
shepherd

THE NEW
TESTAMENT
PASTOR

ROBERT E. PICIRILLI

TEACHER LEADER *shepherd*

THE NEW TESTAMENT PASTOR

ROBERT E. PICIRILLI

randall house

Randall House Publications | Nashville, Tennessee | www.RandallHouse.com

Teacher, Leader, Shepherd: The New Testament Pastor
By Robert E. Picirilli
Published by Randall House Publications
114 Bush Road / Nashville, Tennessee 37217

To request permission to reprint contact:
Permissions
Randall House Publications
114 Bush Road
Nashville, TN 37217

Printed in the United States of America
10-ISBN 0892655690
13-ISBN 9780892655694

Table of CONTENTS

FOREWORD

For some time I have thought about expounding what the New Testament has to say about the pastor. Recently I was invited to speak to my home association of churches, where I was ordained to the ministry, about the pastor's character and calling. In preparing for one of the messages I did an exegetical study of 1 Timothy 3:1-7, and that served to get me started on this project.

I do not propose, here, to tell the minister how to preach, or to describe how the pastor should go about his work, or to treat the practical problems the pastor has to deal with. There are many books on such subjects, some of them very good. I will focus, instead, on understanding what the Bible has to say to or about the pastor and his ministry, treating the passages in the New Testament that speak specifically to the role of the pastor. Primarily, this will be exegetical, though I will include practical exposition of the implications of the biblical text. My hope is that this will contribute to a greater appreciation for, and application of, the biblical teachings about the role of the pastor.

There are also many books available that treat the pastor's office from the perspective of leadership or management theory. Often these reflect what can be learned from observing successful leaders in any field: their techniques, methods, and the like. I do not disrespect such material; it can be very helpful. But our *first* need is to lay a solid foundation for our concept of the pastor's role by setting forth what the Lord Himself has to say about it. Even the veteran pastor can benefit from such a study. Every candidate for a pastoral ministry will, I trust, find this work to be informing and challenging, helping to point his understanding in the right direction.

Primarily, I will include biblical data from passages that refer to *elders*, *bishops*, and *pastors*. There are differences of opinion among interpreters of the Bible and church historians whether these three nouns refer to the same office, just as there are very different concepts about church government. Not all scholars agree as to how the leadership offices in the churches of Acts and the New Testament epistles were structured. My purpose in this work, however, does not include giving attention to such issues. I will proceed on the assumption that every New Testament passage addressed to elders or bishops (overseers) is directly applicable to pastors,[1] that all the principles of leadership set forth in these passages must guide the pastor first of all. Though I personally minister among those who practice congregational (rather than presbyterian or episcopal) church government, I believe that these principles will apply to pastors in any context.

I also write as one who believes in a divinely-called ministry, for others who hold that same view—and these have been many in the history of the church. Consequently I will not so much argue for this position as assume it. I will likewise assume the position, which is dominant in my own denomination, that the pastoral ministry is intended for men—as appears to be required by 1 Timothy 2:12.[2] Even so, whatever one's views on these matters, what the New Testament says to those who serve as pastors will apply.

---

[1] This is true even if the bishop-pastor was one among a plurality of "elders," as some interpreters hold.

[2] I say this with full awareness that some women have made important contributions to my denomination, and to many others, as preachers or even as pastors.

I first thought to offer chapters on each of the passages that speak about the pastor's work and then to draw out practical implications. With that in mind I proceeded to exegete each passage. But this resulted in a great deal of repetition, given that many of the passages share the same teachings. So I decided, instead, to take a more thematic approach and offer a succession of chapters on various aspects of the pastor's call, qualifications, and role. Even so, I trust that the reader will see that the discussion is entirely grounded in exegesis of the several passages. Following this preface, these passages are printed, together with a brief exegetical outline and a pointer to the chapters that will give more attention to them. Scripture quotations are generally from the New King James Version (NKJV), but I have tried to make sure that those who are more familiar with the King James (KJV) wording will find the material equally usable.

A word about the system of documentation used herein: I did not want to clutter the pages with footnotes that give only bibliographical information about the sources cited. Instead, I have noted sources as briefly as possible within the text: the author's last name, or an abbreviation for a reference work, and a page number in parentheses. The reader who desires to check out the source has only to look in the bibliography in the back to find all the information needed for accurate identification. This means, then, that footnotes actually includedon the pages include additional observations or information.

I am grateful to Dr. Paul Harrison, an active pastor, and to the Rev. Matthew Pinson, president of Free Will Baptist Bible College, for reading a not-quite-final draft of this book. Though neither of them will agree with everything I say, both have graciously offered helpful comments and suggestions—some of which I have followed!

THE NEW TESTAMENT MATERIAL

1 TIMOTHY 3:1-7

1 This *is* a faithful saying, If a man desires the position of a bishop, he desires a good work.

2 A bishop then must be blameless, the husband of one wife, temperate, sober-minded, of good behavior, hospitable, able to teach;

3 not given to wine, not violent, not greedy for money; but gentle, not quarrelsome, not covetous;

4 one who rules his ow house well, having *his* children in submission with all reverence

5 (for if a man does not know how to rule his own house, how will he take care of the church of God?);

6 not a novice, lest being puffed up with pride he fall into the *same* condemnation as the devil.

7 Moreover he must have a good testimony among those who are outside, lest he fall into reproach and the snare of the devil.

Exegetical Outline

1. The Position or Role of Pastor
  1.1. "The position of bishop," v. 1
  1.2. "Able to teach," v. 2
  1.3. "Take care of the church of God," v. 5

2. The Pastor's Call
  2.1. The candidate's perspective, v. 1
  2.2. The church's perspective, vv. 2-7

3. The Pastor's Qualifications
  3.1. Positive qualifications, vv. 2-5,7: blameless, husband of one wife, temperate, sober-minded, of good behavior, hospitable, able to teach, gentle, one that rules well his own house, having a good testimony among those outside
  3.2. Negative qualifications, vv. 2, 3, 6: not given to wine, not violent, not greedy for money, not quarrelsome, not covetous, not a novice

See chapters 1-7

5 For this reason I left you in Crete, that you should set in order the things that are lacking, and appoint elders in every city, as I commanded you—

6 if a man is blameless, the husband of one wife, having faithful children not accused of dissipation or insubordination.

7 For a bishop must be blameless, as a steward of God; not self-willed, not quick-tempered, not given to wine, not violent, not greedy for money,

8 but hospitable, a lover of what is good, sober-minded, just, holy, self-controlled,

9 holding fast the faithful word as he has been taught, that he may be able, by sound doctrine, both to exhort and convict those who contradict.

1. The Ordaining of Elders, v. 1

2. General Qualifications for All Elders, v. 6: "... blameless, the husband of one wife, with faithful children not accused of dissipation or insubordination."

3. Specific Qualifications for the Bishop/Pastor, vv. 7-9: "... not self-willed, not quick-tempered, not given to wine, not violent, not greedy for money, hospitable, a lover of what is good, sober-minded, just, holy, self-controlled, holding fast the faithful word as he has been taught, able by sound doctrine both to exhort and to convict those who contradict."

See chapters 1, 3, 4, 5

1 PETER 5:1-4

1 The elders who are among you I exhort, I who am a fellow elder and a witness of the sufferings of Christ, and also a partaker of the glory that will be revealed:

2 Shepherd the flock of God which is among you, serving as overseers, not by constraint but willingly, not for dishonest gain but eagerly;

3 nor as being lords over those entrusted to you, but being examples to the flock;

4 and when the Chief Shepherd appears, you will receive the crown of glory that does not fade away.

Exegetical Outline

1. The Pastor's Work, v. 2
   1.1. Shepherding the flock of God
   1.2. Exercising oversight

2. The Pastor's Motives and Manner, vv. 2, 3
   2.1. Not by constraint but willingly
   2.2. Not for dishonest gain but eagerly
   2.3. Not as being lords over but being examples to the flock

3. The Pastor's Reward, v. 4

See chapters 1, 2, 6

ACTS 20:28-31

28 Therefore take heed to yourselves and to all the flock, among which the Holy Spirit has made you overseers, to shepherd the church of God, which He purchased with His own blood.

29 For I know this, that after my departure savage wolves will come in among you, not sparing the flock.

30 Also from among yourselves men will rise up, speaking perverse things, to draw away the disciples after themselves.

31 Therefore watch, and remember that for three years I did not cease to warn everyone night and day with tears.

Exegetical Outline

1. The Pastor's Realm of Responsibility: The Church as the Flock of God, v. 28

2. The Pastor's Role in the Church: An Overseer to Shepherd the Flock, v. 28

3. The Pastor's Attitude
   3.1. Take heed, v. 28
   3.2. Watch, vv. 29-31

See chapters 1, 6

1 THESSALONIANS 5:12-14

12 And we urge you, brethren, to recognize those who labor among you, and are over you in the Lord and admonish you,

13 and to esteem them very highly in love for their work's sake. Be at peace among yourselves.

14 Now we exhort you, brethren, warn those who are unruly, comfort the faint-hearted, uphold the weak, be patient with all.

Exegetical Outline

1. The Pastor's Responsibilities, v. 12
  1.1. They "labor among you."
  1.2. They "are over you in the Lord."
  1.3. They "admonish you."

2. The Congregation's Response, vv. 12, 13
  2.1. Recognition
  2.2. Esteem
  2.3. Love

3. The Ministry Involved, v. 14

See chapter 7

HEBREWS 13:7, 17, 24

7 Remember those who rule over you, who have spoken the word of God to you, whose faith follow, considering the outcome of *their* conduct.

17 Obey those who rule over you, and be submissive, for they watch out for your souls, as those who must give account. Let them do so with joy and not with grief, for that would be unprofitable for you.

24 Greet all those who rule over you.

Exegetical Outline

1. The Pastor as Leader: "those who rule over you"

2. The Pastor's Leadership Responsibilities:
  2.1. He speaks the Word of God, v. 7
  2.2. He sets an example in faith, v. 7
  2.3. He watches for souls, v. 17

3. The Pastor's Accountability, v. 17

See chapters 5, 7

1 TIMOTHY 5:17-19

17 Let the elders who rule well be counted worthy of double honor, especially those who labor in the word and doctrine.

18 For the Scripture says, "You shall not muzzle an ox while it treads out the grain," and, "The laborer *is* worthy of his wages."

19 Do not receive an accusation against an elder except from two or three witnesses.

Exegetical Outline

1. The Pastor as "ruler"

2. The Pastor as "laboring in the Word and doctrine"

3. The Church's Responsibilities

    3.1. Support for the pastor
    3.2. Respect for the pastor

See chapters 5, 7

EPHESIANS 4:11, 12

11 And He Himself gave some *to be* apostles, some prophets, some evangelists, and some pastors and teachers,

12 for the equipping of the saints for the work of ministry, for the edifying of the body of Christ,

Exegetical Outline

1. The Pastor as Shepherd, v. 11

2. The Pastor as Teacher, v. 11

3. The Pastor's Purpose, v. 12

   3.1. Intermediate purpose: equip the saints for ministry
   3.2. Ultimate purpose: the edification of the body of Christ

See chapters 1, 5, 6

BIBLICAL TERMS THAT APPLY
TO THE OFFICE OF PASTOR

Acts 14:23: [Paul and Barnabas] "*appointed elders in every church.*"

Acts 20:17, 28: "From Miletus he sent to Ephesus and called for the elders of the church." [And Paul said to them,] "Therefore take heed to yourselves and to all the flock, among which the Holy Spirit has made you overseers."

Ephesians 4:11: "And he himself gave some to be . . . pastors and teachers."

1 Timothy 3:1, 2: "If a man desires the position of a bishop, he desires a good work. A bishop then must be blameless."

Titus 1:5, 7: [Paul to Titus: I left you in Crete] "that you should . . . appoint elders in every city . . . . For a bishop must be blameless."

1 Peter 5:1, 2: "The elders who are among you I exhort . . . Shepherd the flock of God which is among you, serving as overseers."

The three primary terms used in the New Testament that apply directly to the person we call pastor are *elder, bishop,* and *pastor.*

As noted in the Foreword, I am proceeding on the assumption that everything in the New Testament addressed to "bishops" or "elders" also speaks to pastors.

My purpose in this work is to examine in detail what the New Testament says about the office of pastor, whether identified by one of these three terms or when neither term is used and the role is referred to indirectly. This chapter focuses on the meaning of the three terms, which give insight into the nature of the pastor's work. As John Wesley asked, and answered: "Is there any hope that a man should discharge his office well, if he knows not what it is? . . . Nay, if he knows not the work God has given him to do, he cannot finish it" (10.482).

1. ELDER

There is a consensus view that the earliest New Testament churches were organized under the leadership of *elders*, following a pattern of organization the first (Jewish) Christians were already familiar with in their synagogues. Apparently the first use of this term within the fledgling church is in Acts 11:30 and refers to elders among the Jerusalem believers, likewise named several times in Acts 15 in the phrase, "the apostles and elders" (see verses 2, 4, 6, 22, 23).

The Pauline churches had elders. In Acts 14:21 we learn that Paul and Barnabas completed their first missionary journey by making a return visit to the churches they had planted in Lystra, Iconium, and Antioch. As they did so they "appointed elders in every church"[3] (14:23). In Acts 20, Paul summoned the *elders* of the Ephesian church to meet him in Miletus.

Paul's letters give attention to the place of elders. He instructed Titus, for example, to "appoint elders in every city" (1:5). In 1 Timothy 5:17 he urged that elders who rule well be given "double honor."

Peter and James likewise refer to elders. James 5:14 urges ailing believers to "call for the elders of the church" to anoint and pray for them. First Peter 5:1 addresses "the elders who are among you."[4]

Applying the term *elder* to the pastor has some important implications. The Greek word is *presbuteros* and it first has the natural meaning of an *older* person. In Acts 2:17, for example, it stands in contrast to "young men"; likewise in 1 Timothy 5:1. Then it apparently came to mean a person who has the defined status of "elder," a term chosen to indicate persons with maturity and selected for official responsibilities. While no certain age for the office is stated, no doubt the basic concept involved persons who were truly older and experienced. Older people were highly regarded in that culture. Karen Jobes (302) thinks of the earliest elders as "leaders . . . who were probably heads of households where house churches met," but the role "became more formalized and official as the needs of the churches developed." She may be right in this, but we cannot be sure; nor does this matter for the purpose of this work.

---

[3] Some read this to mean *one* elder for each church, others of plural elders for each congregation; Stott (*1 Timothy & Titus* 174), commenting on the use of *elders* in the pastoral letters, says, "This might mean a single elder in each house-church . . . . [or] that there were several presbyters in each church." Either way, the principle of congregational church government is not contradicted.

[4] Both of these letters were written to multiple churches, so it is again possible that each church had but one "elder" or that each had plural elders; see note 1, pg viii.

The pastor is certainly an elder, and the title itself makes clear that the pastor has a position of respect and responsibility. He has status in the congregation. Furthermore, maturity and experience are part of the job description. The qualifications discussed in chapters three and four will make this even clearer.

2. BISHOP = OVERSEER

In 1 Timothy 3:1, five English words—"the position of a bishop" ("the office of a bishop," KJV)—represent just one Greek word, *episcopē*. It has the same root as the word translated "bishop" in verse 2 (*episcopos*) and so refers to the position or work of the person who wears that title. There is also a verb on the same root, *episkopeō*, which means (in this context) to exercise the office, to function as a bishop or overseer.

Technically, neither "office" nor "position" is explicitly part of the Greek word, which works the same way as when we adapt our English word *president* by referring to his office as the *presidency*, or when we speak of the place a *pastor* fills as the *pastorate*. There is no English word like "bishopcy" or "bishopate," of course, but that is the idea. In Acts 1:20, when the eleven apostles were discussing the need to name a twelfth man to take Judas's place, they quoted the words of Psalm 69:25, "Let another take his *office*" (KJV, *bishoprick*), the very word used in 1 Timothy.

Obviously, then, "the position of a bishop" means the place filled by a bishop, the role and responsibilities involved in the bishop's ministry. The important question for us is what this means, and although etymology isn't always a sure guide to the meaning of a word, we may start there. *Episcopeō* is a combination of the preposition *epi*, upon or over, and the verb *skopeo*, to watch, look, or see. This appears to picture a bishop as one who watches over, looks out for, or oversees; the lexicographers generally agree that this is indeed the meaning of the word.

Consequently, many versions translate the word by *overseer*. In 1 Timothy 3:1 the NIV reads, "If anyone sets his heart *on being an overseer*." The NASB reads, "If any man aspires to *the office of overseer*." Even the KJV translates the plural noun as "overseers" in Acts 20:28. This has the advantage of avoiding the special usage of *bishop* to refer not to an ordinary pastor, for example, but to an elite clergyman who has authority over pastors—as the word is used in denominations (like the Methodist and Episcopal churches) that are governed by a hierarchy of bishops.[5] The word is never used that way in the New Testament.

But even *overseer* may have some disadvantages as a translation, since it seems to suggest that the primary function of the office is to exercise authority over, to *supervise*.[6] The fundamental question about this word, then, is its primary focus. Even by its etymology, *episkopeō* can mean to "watch over" as much as to "oversee."

Most scholars of the language will agree, I think, that the basic meaning of this word is *to exercise watch-care over*. This involves supervisory oversight, to be sure, and the "overseer-ship" (as we might render in 1 Timothy 3:1) is without doubt a position of

---

[5] We call this an *episcopal* form of church government, as opposed to a *presbyterian* form (governed by a body of elders) or to *congregational* church government (governed by the congregation as a whole).

[6] *Supervise* is from Latin roots and has the same etymological meaning as *episkopeō* in Greek.

authority. Indeed, the word was sometimes applied to "governors (in colonies), to certain magistrates (in autonomous cities)" or to other "high-ranking functionaries" (Spicq 2.51). The primary responsibility of the person who bears this title is to look out for the welfare of the church entrusted to his watch-care.

A Greek lexicon, therefore, defines the word as "one who has the responsibility of caring for spiritual concerns — 'one responsible for, one who cares for, guardian, keeper,'" or "one who serves as a leader in a church — 'church leader'" (*LN* 1.463, 542). The editors add that "it is important to try to combine the concepts of both service and leadership, in other words, the responsibility of *caring for* the needs of a congregation as well as *directing* the activities of the membership" (italics added). I am satisfied that this observation catches the true meaning of the word; it is based on an analysis of the uses of the word in the New Testament and in other Greek literature of the period.

Beyond this basic understanding, of course, we must determine the precise nature of the office from the things that are said about it in the New Testament; that is the purpose of this entire work. At this point, then, we simply consider the way the three words that share this Greek root are used in the New Testament, our primary and authoritative source for understanding things biblical.

1. The verb *episkopeō*, meaning to exercise this watch-care responsibility, occurs only twice. In Hebrews 12:15 it apparently does not refer to the formal office we are discussing, but to every believer's responsibility to "look diligently" or *watch out* that no one fails of the grace of God. In 1 Peter 5:2, 3, however, it ap-

parently refers to the official responsibility of a bishop or overseer to "exercise watch-care" over the flock of God, and to do so not as "exercising lordship" over them but as examples. Peter defines this overseeing watch-care as including the responsibility to "shepherd" the flock. (All elements of this passage will be treated in subsequent chapters.)

2. The noun of office, *episkopē*, meaning the position of oversight or watch-care, occurs four times in the New Testament. In two of them (Lk. 19:44; 1 Pet. 2:12) the word means a "visitation" and has no bearing on the discussion here. In Acts 1:20, mentioned above, it refers to Judas's apostolic office. In 1 Timothy 3:1, as cited above, the word means "the office of a bishop" as discussed above.

3. The noun of person, *episkopos*, meaning the one who has this position, appears five times. In addition to 1 Timothy 3:2 there is also the parallel Titus 1:7. In Philippians 1:1 the word occurs when Paul addresses his letter to "all the saints in Christ Jesus which are at Philippi, with the *bishops* and deacons," a twofold distinction of titles matching 1 Timothy 3.

In Acts 20:28, as mentioned already, the word occurs in an instructive passage: "Therefore take heed to yourselves and to all the flock, among which the Holy Spirit has made you overseers, to shepherd the church of God, which He purchased with His own blood." "Made you overseers" is, literally, "placed [*tithēmi*] you [as] overseers," obviously focusing on the Lord's primary role in bringing the person to such a position. As Calvin (19.1.254) comments, "Paul standeth principally upon this, that they were not appointed by men, but the charge of the Church was committed unto them by

God" (*CSB*). Chrysostom makes the point, "See, it is from the Spirit ye have your ordination" (*NPNF1* 11.269).

Spicq (2.52) appropriately observes, "Not only does the *episkopos* watch over and busy himself with the community, but he also sees to its spiritual needs and devotes all his energy to it."

3. PASTOR-TEACHER

It seems clear that *bishop* or *overseer* in the New Testament corresponds to the person we call *pastor*. While I will not pursue all the details that justify this equation of terms, I will at least summarize the major considerations involved. If they refer to the same person, it is likely that *bishop* or *overseer* was the more official title, with *pastor* reflecting his spiritual gift and allegorizing his function as a shepherd. Homer Kent (117, 118) thinks "pastor-teacher" was the name of the spiritual gift given by Christ rather than the name of a formal office within the church.

The English term *pastor* means a *shepherd*. Whenever "pastor" appears in the New Testament, or in other English literature of the period, "shepherd" would be an equally correct translation, and vice versa. The King James translators (like others before and since) chose "pastor" for the very reason that in their usage of the English language it was another word for a shepherd.[7]

The Greek word is *poimēn*, usually rendered "shepherd" and usually referring to literal shepherds (as in Lk. 2:8, 15, etc.). Sometimes it is used of Jesus Christ (Heb. 13:20; 1 Pet. 2:25; and

---

[7] Even today, a "pastoral" scene is usually one involving a shepherd or sheep. Had Psalm 23 read "The Lord is my *pastor*," that would have been entirely appropriate in the English culture of the time.

allegorically in Jn. 10:11). Only once in the English New Testament is *poimēn* translated *pastor* in anything like our sense of the word (Ephesians 4:11). There it refers to one of the gifts given by the victorious, ascending Christ to His church: namely, the gift of "pastors and teachers." The wording (both in Greek and in English) makes almost certain that these two words identify the same gift: "pastor" views the office by the analogy of a "shepherd" with a flock, and "teacher" identifies the office in terms of the primary work involved—teaching the Word of God.[8]

Acts 20:28 contributes to the understanding that bishop and pastor are names for the same office. There Paul addresses the elders he had summoned (Acts 20:17): "Therefore take heed to yourselves and to all the flock, among which the Holy Spirit has made you overseers, to shepherd the church of God, which He purchased with His own blood." *Overseers* is *episkopoi*, "bishops."[9] And "feed" is the verb *poimainō*, literally "to shepherd," the verb form of the same root as the noun *poimēn*, "shepherd, pastor." They are bishops or overseers for the purpose of "shepherding" the flock. First Peter 2:25 makes the equation of the two terms even clearer, referring to Jesus Christ as "the Shepherd [*poimēn*, Pastor] and Overseer [*episkopos*] of your souls"; as Spicq observes, the expression is no doubt an instance of "hendiadys,"[10] which he renders as "guardian Shepherd" (1.207, n. 8).

---

[8] I am aware that a few interpreters do not take the words as names for the same function; see further discussion in chapter five.

[9] Based on this, Kent (117-20) equates the terms *bishop* and *elder* and affirms that the church at Ephesus, at least, had plural bishops. Even so, he thinks the "closest modern equivalent is the pastor" (118), whom he consistently refers to as singular.

[10] *Hendiadys* ("one through two") is a figure of speech in which two nouns have the same meaning as a single noun with a modifying adjective.

The verb *poimainō*, "to shepherd," is used again in 1 Peter 5:2, also translated "*feed* the flock of God" in the KJV but with a broader meaning that encompasses all the duties of the shepherd in exercising watch-care over the sheep. Most lexicons and commentators today will urge that it means to tend or care for people as a shepherd tends a flock of sheep. This is the way Jesus apparently meant the word in John 21:16 when he said to Peter, "Feed (*poimainō*—tend/shepherd) my sheep" (KJV).

The idea of the "pastor" leads in the same direction, then, as the discussion of the word *episkopos* above; the focus is on giving watch-care. To be sure, a shepherd is a leader and exercises authority over the flock; that idea is important. The ancient Jewish writer Philo said, "The shepherd's mission is so lofty that it is rightly attributed not only to kings, sages, and souls of perfect purity, but even to the Lord God" (*Husbandry* 50, cited in Spicq 1.206). Compare Psalm 23:1. Indeed, the king of Israel was appropriately identified as the nation's *shepherd*; see Psalm 78:70-72 for the background of this usage. Other sovereigns in the East were often called shepherd or pastor (Spicq 1.206).

Although the word applies to one who exercises ruling authority, the primary focus of the term itself is on his broad responsibility as a shepherd to look out for—care for, guard, tend, exercise watch-care, feed, supervise, meet the needs of—the flock "among which" God has placed him. "A shepherd is responsible for the total well-being of the flock" (Hillyer 139).

IMPLICATIONS FOR PRACTICAL APPLICATION

Some things are clear already, even though we have focused only on the terms that can indicate the pastor, including *teacher, bishop* or *overseer*, and *elder*. As an elder, he must be a person of maturity and experience. One reason for this will become clear in 1 Timothy 3:6, when we examine the pastor's qualifications; see chapter four. The very title *elder* implies that it is a position of respect, and one who has not proved himself can hardly expect to have that. It also implies he has responsibility, and in no field of endeavor should a person be given such responsibility who has not grown into it through prior experience.

The primary focus of the other titles is on the pastor's responsibility to exercise a shepherd-like watch-care over the congregation to which he ministers, viewing the church by analogy as the "flock" of God. This especially includes his responsibility to teach them the Word of God. Subsequent chapters will also develop this emphasis, especially chapters five and six. Meanwhile, by definition, no man is qualified as pastor who lacks a shepherd's heart. "The [shepherd] metaphor suggests watchfulness, care, benevolence, and devotion" (Spicq 1.206, n. 5).

This seems the best place to emphasize that Paul calls this role "a good work" (1 Tim. 3:1); as J. N. D. Kelly (72) renders, he "sets his heart on a worthwhile job." George Knight (155) calls attention to the fact that "a number of the early church fathers stress that it is a *work* and not a *dignity* or an *exalted position*." Augustine (*City of God* 19.19) was among these; commenting on 1 Timothy 3:1 he observed that Paul "wanted to make clear that the office of bishop . . . implies work rather than dignity" (*ACCS* 9.169). The Puritan William Gurnall (2.546) said: "He that preaches as he should, shall find it a work, not a play. Not a work of an hour while speaking in the pulpit, but a load that lies heavy on his shoulders all the week long" (*CSB*).

In a slightly different vein Mounce (169) comments that it is a good work "because the overseer is instrumental in helping the church protect the truth of the gospel." The fourth-century Greek expositor Chrysostom emphasized that the bishop's work is "a work of protection. If anyone has this desire, so that he does not covet the dominion and authority, but wishes to protect the Church, I blame him not" (*NPNF1* 13.437).

The titles alone impress on us the importance of the role of pastor. He is a respected elder with maturity and experience. He is a shepherd, a person who exercises oversight and watch-care over a church as the flock of God. This includes, especially, his responsibility to teach them the Word of God. There is no greater honor and no weightier responsibility than this.

CHAPTER 2

THE PASTOR'S CALL

1 Timothy 3:1: "If a man desires the position of a bishop, he desires a good work."

Titus 1:5: "Appoint elders in every city."

1 Peter 5:2: "Shepherd the flock of God which is among you, serving as overseers, not by constraint but willingly, not for dishonest gain but eagerly;"

Martyn Lloyd-Jones (9) speaks for many when he insists that "the work of preaching is the highest and the greatest and the most glorious calling to which anyone can ever be called." He acknowledges (104) that defining such a call is "not an easy matter," but he describes it in typical terms as beginning with "a consciousness within one's own spirit" recognized as "God dealing with you" and confirmed "through the influence of others" and a developing "concern about others" that leads to "a desire to do something" about "their lost estate and condition."

These days, however, some Christian leaders downplay the idea of the call to the ministry. Some of their reasons have some validity. For example, they do not want young men waiting for some overwhelming supernatural experience, some audible voice in the night, something that knocks them down on the Damascus Road. Furthermore, they do not want the church to be left out, limited to the subjectivity of one man's inner feeling or claim.

In my view, as in much of the church (including the tradition I represent), one may uphold the idea that men are called by God to the pastoral ministry without yielding to such abuses. All that is needed is to define the "call" in biblical terms. I am impressed that the passages that speak to the pastor help us do that.

1. 1 TIMOTHY 3:1-7 AND THE TWO SIDES OF THE CALL

My reading of this passage suggests that the biblical call to be a pastor has two sides. On the one hand, verse 1 refers explicitly to the man's *desire*. That reflects the subjective side. On the other hand, the rest of the passage emphasizes even more strongly the qualifications that the *church* must take into account before issuing its own call. That reflects the objective side. Both the man and the church must acknowledge the call of a person to pastor. Even Lloyd-Jones, who emphasizes the subjective side, insists (108) that the man's "personal call must be confirmed by the Church." Again he remarks (114), "God works through the man himself and through the voice of the Church."

It is not a credit to the ministry for an ordaining council to ask a candidate, "Brother, has God called you to preach?" and then, on being convinced of his sincerity, to ordain him without further ado. It is not enough for a man to feel called.[11] He needs to demonstrate to the satisfaction of the church that the Lord of the church intends him to be pastor. *Both God and the church issue the call to the ministry of pastoring!* And I do not think this is heresy: why else would we say that a church "calls" a pastor?[12]

In his discussion of "vocational decision-making" Packer (57) correctly observes: "Self-judgments have to be judged and checked by others. When God calls, he equips; when the equipment is lacking, and the potential for role fulfillment is simply not there, God's call is not to what the candidate had in mind, but to something else. And it is within the body [of Christ] that each person's true calling will be discerned" (*CSB*).

Even so, we need not downplay the subjective side, and this requires that we give closer examination to verse 1. As already seen in chapter one, the verse identifies what all this is about: namely, the office or position of a bishop, the "overseership" of a church. If a man desires the responsibility of looking out for the church, of exercising watch-care over the church—that is the meaning of the words.

Desire occurs twice in this verse: if a man *desires* this responsibility, this role, he *desires* a good work, says Paul. These are two different Greek words, both of them strong and interesting words, neither one the usual word for desire in the New Testament.

---

[11] The old joke about the fellow who saw "G P" in the clouds and took it to mean "go preach"—only later to learn that it must have meant "go plow"—is not entirely foolishness!

[12] It will be obvious, I think, that I am not so much concerned with what is termed the "call to preach" as with the call to be a pastor of a local church.

The first is *oregomai*. Etymologically it means to reach or stretch out for, and so in actual usage it means "to eagerly desire to accomplish some goal or purpose—'to strive to attain, to aspire to, to eagerly long for'" (*LN* 1.291). It only occurs twice more in the New Testament. One of these is Hebrews 11:16 where we read that the Old Testament patriarchs *desire* or *long for* a better—that is, a heavenly—country. The other is 1 Timothy 6:10 with its warning that some people, *desiring* money, have strayed from the faith.

The other word is *epithumeō*, frequently translated "lust," usually in a bad sense in the New Testament: illicit sexual passion (Mt. 5:28) or desire for material things (Acts 20:33, "covet"). But it can be a good desire or passion also, as it is here: "to long for, to desire very much" (*LN* 1.290); Matthew 13:17 is one of several examples of an approved desire.

The point in 1 Timothy is: "This godly desire for the responsible task of overseership, if controlled by the Spirit of God, may deepen into a sacred conviction" (Kent 119). God puts in the heart of some a passion to serve in the ministry, a reaching out to serve as overseer, shepherd, pastor of the flock of God, an eager desire for the responsibility of watch-care over the church. It seems to me that when God puts such a desire in a man this is the call, at least from its subjective side. No one else can immediately sense or feel that calling; it is God's work in the heart of the pastor-to-be.

Interestingly, this desire is not mentioned in other passages that speak of the appointment of pastors. The reason, apparently, is that those passages do not undertake to enlighten us regarding man's subjective awareness. Instead, they typically speak either from the church's or from God's perspective. In Acts 14:23, for example, we simply learn that Paul and Barnabas led the church in setting aside elders. In Titus 1:5 Paul instructs his associate to appoint elders in the churches and lists qualifications. Ephesians 4:11 presents only the perspective of Christ's gift of pastors to the church. Acts 20:28 focuses on the Holy Spirit's activity in putting the overseers in place. In 1 Peter 5 the writer addresses those who are already elders. Neither passage undertakes to represent the candidate's perspective at all—which by no means requires that the man have no perspective! Only 1 Timothy 3 pulls back the curtain and gives us a glimpse of the man's own understanding before he becomes pastor. And it describes his *desire*, which I read as evidence of the work of the Holy Spirit within.

The question may arise, of course, whether every man called to pastor must necessarily have this strong desire. Is it possible, for example, for a church to recognize the gift and calling of God for an individual before the man himself? Though the New Testament does not answer these questions for us, our experiences in the church tend to say that the church, indeed, may recognize God's intention for a man before he does. And we have heard of men who have not sought the pastorate but have been brought into "the ministry," at least, by the church's initiative. One of my great mentors, for example, enjoyed relating his personal experience in this regard. Though he felt no inner "call" his pastor and others urged him in that direction, gave him opportunities to preach, and asked to ordain him. In light of their confidence he acceded to *their* desire. Still, when he was later asked to become a Bible college president, he wrestled with whether that work would be in accord with his call to preach.

I take it as significant, then, that Paul speaks of a man's *desire*—without necessarily eliminating some other evidence of God's calling. Indeed, though the crucial clause in 1 Timothy 3:1 is an "if" clause, it is not a clause of mere possibility; instead, it has the perspective of something assumed true.[13] I tend to believe, then, that Paul's expression is the typical evidence of calling on the part of the man himself. And I tend to believe that unless that desire to serve as pastor arises *at some point* within the man himself, a church would be wise to require overwhelming evidence of God's call before inviting him to serve as its pastor.[14] Furthermore, it seems to me that Peter's discussion of the pastor's *motives* (see point 3) also represents this same perspective; he fairly insists that the elders serve with eager desire.

2. TITUS 1:5-9 AND THE ORDAINING OF ELDERS

Paul instructs Titus to "appoint elders in every city, as I commanded you" (v. 5). This apparently means that elders are to be formally put in place. Calvin (21.2.290) said that "churches cannot safely remain without the ministry of pastors, and that consequently, wherever there is a considerable body of people, a pastor should be appointed over it" (*CSB*).

The verb used here is *kathistēmi*, "to assign to someone a position of authority over others—'to put in charge of, to appoint, to designate'" (*LN* 1.484). By itself, the word does not necessarily

---

[13] It is a "first class condition" in Greek.

[14] Again, one should note that I am referring to the call to a pastorate, not to "ordination to the Gospel ministry" in general.

imply a formal "ordination" ceremony of any sort, only that such persons were to be installed in office. Titus was thus to *constitute* elders in the churches, city by city.

As noted in chapter one, Acts 14:23 also refers to this as something Paul and Barnabas did in the churches planted during the first missionary journey: they "appointed" elders in every church. Only there a different verb is used: *cheirotoneō*, "to formally appoint or assign someone to a particular task—'to appoint, to assign'" (*LN* 1.484). Sometimes the verb, more simply, meant to "choose, select," as in 2 Corinthians 8:19, its only other occurrence in the New Testament. But when the action is a formal one, it amounts to an official appointment, and so the two verbs in Titus and 2 Corinthians are essentially synonyms.

This is not the place for a discussion of ordination procedures. Indeed, the New Testament itself does not describe such procedures. The point is that, regardless of how it is done, pastors should be formally appointed to office and thus "ordained." As discussed above, this means that the man's "calling" to the pastorate is in this way issued by the church.

Ordination is not "sacramental" in a formal sense: that is, it does not represent the conveying of some special power or rights on the person ordained; it does not provide the person with automatic authority to "rule" a congregation, an authority that can only come from the congregation itself.[15] Ordination is therefore recognition by the church that the person manifests the qualifications and desire

---

[15] In the congregational system of church government, all authority in the church (other than that of God and His Word, of course) ultimately resides in the local congregation. In traditions that function differently, ordination may have a different basis but is nonetheless important.

that give evidence of God's call to ministerial service. It signifies the church's acceptance of that person for such service and in effect sets him apart with its blessing.[16]

In the tradition I am most familiar with, churches delegate to wider associations of churches the responsibility for formal ordination to the ministry.[17] I have no desire to evaluate that here; no doubt there are some things about this practice that are good and some that are not so good. Regardless, whether at the local church level or in cooperation with other churches, the church must carefully examine a man before ordaining him to the ministry. After all, regardless of his formal ordination, the local church has the final word; it must actively satisfy itself that a man is qualified before issuing its pastoral call to him. As I have implied already, being an ordained preacher is not quite the same thing as being pastor in a specific church.

3. 1 PETER 5:1-4 AND THE PASTOR'S MOTIVES

In evaluating whether a man is truly "called" to a pastoral ministry, we must take into account what motivates him. Sometimes what appears to be a God-given "desire" is something else entirely. John Wesley (10.494) insisted that pastors ask themselves a telling question: "What was my intention in taking upon me this office and ministry? Was it always, and is it now, wholly and solely to glorify God, and save souls?"

---

[16] For a helpful discussion of ordination among Southern Baptists, see the discussion by Lea (141-44) along with the other sources he references.

[17] This is not 100% true, but even when ordination is sponsored by a local church other ministers or churches in the fellowship are formally involved in some way. One way or another, cooperative efforts are appropriate for churches joined in associations. They represent concerns for the church abroad, concerns that reach beyond the bounds of a local church.

When Peter speaks, in this passage, to his fellow elders, he urges them to "feed" (KJV)—tend, shepherd—the flock of God and "exercise oversight" in doing this. This will be discussed in chapter six under the heading of the pastor as shepherd. But here seems the best place to discuss two of the three "not this, but this" phrases (1 Pet. 5:2, 3) that describe the motives and manner of the pastor's ministry.

Technically, these phrases qualify the participle "exercising oversight"; but for all practical purposes they modify both this participle and the commanding verb "shepherd the flock of God." I will deal with the third phrase, which speaks to the *manner* of the man's ministry, in chapter six, the pastor as shepherd. The first two are important for our understanding of the pastor's call since they address his *motives* for being in the ministry in the first place.

1. *Not by constraint but willingly.* Some who read these words may think they refer to the authority the pastor exercises over the congregation: that is, he must not "constrain" them but enlist them willingly. That, however, is clearly not the point. Instead, it refers to the nature of the pastor's choice to serve: *he* must not be a pastor because he has been "constrained" but must do so "willingly." As indicated in 1 Timothy 3:1, discussed above, the inward call typically produces a *desire* for the work; the willingness referred to here goes hand in hand with that.

"By constraint" is the adverb *anankastōs*, which means "by compulsion" or "as a matter of obligation." This is the word's only appearance in the New Testament, but a verb on the same stem (*anankazō*, compel; Gal. 2:14), an adjective (*anankaios*, necessary;

1 Cor. 12:22), and an abstract noun (*anankē*, compulsion, necessity; 1 Cor. 9:16) also occur.

"Willingly" is the adverb *hekousiōs*, obviously the opposite of by compulsion: "voluntarily"—or even "intentionally," as in its only other New Testament appearance in Hebrews 10:26 ("willfully"). The related adjective *hekousios* occurs only in Philemon 14, where it stands in contrast to the same word as here. Indeed, that passage provides a good illustration of the difference: Paul desired that Philemon's response to his appeal on Onesimus's behalf be voluntary and not by compulsion.[18] "The task must be carried out 'willingly,' i.e., not only out of the joy connected with such work, but also because one has placed oneself willingly at the disposal of the God whose concerns are, after all, at stake here" (Goppelt 345).

A number of early manuscripts have here the additional words *kata theon*: literally, "according to God" (NASB: "according to the will of God"). Whether this was original or not, its point is to qualify the "willingly" in a way that the context justifies even if the phrase is not expressed. In other words, the decision to be a pastor is not *absolutely* voluntary; it is not a matter of *self*-will. The man must have the assurance that this is in accord with *God's* will for him. He has the desire and enters the pastoral ministry willingly; no one, including the church, forces the office on him; he senses that this is God's call. The NIV captures the meaning well: "not because you must, but because you are willing, as God wants you to be."

---

[18] A related verbal adjective is in 1 Corinthians 9:17 and Romans 8:20.

In other words, the man who becomes a pastor should not do so as a result of being compelled or forced into the position; he should do this voluntarily, of his own free will, and yet in compliance with the will of God. This may well be the reconciliation (if one is needed) between Paul's own personal sense of necessity and willingness in preaching the gospel (1 Cor. 9:16, 17), where precisely the same words are used. "Begrudging service is not to be offered, for leadership so motivated will ultimately not be pleasing to God" (Jobes 304).

2. *Not for dishonest gain, but eagerly.* This also refers to the pastor's motives. "For dishonest gain" (KJV, "For filthy lucre") is the adverb *aischrokerdōs*, on the same stem as the adjective used in 1 Timothy 3:3, 8 and Titus 1:7, discussed in treating the qualifications of the pastor as given in those passages (chapter four). It might mean to be greedy for what can be gained shamefully or to be shamefully greedy; both wind up at the same place. The motivation for a pastor's ministry must not be greed and he must not seek gain in any shameful manner but must always act with integrity and in a way that is completely aboveboard.

"Eagerly" (KJV, "of a ready mind") is the adverb *prothumōs*, whose meaning is nearly synonymous with *hekousiōs* ("willingly"), just above. But Louw and Nida (*LN* 1.297) warn that we must not precisely equate the two since *prothumōs* implies "far more desire and eagerness." They explain that the difference, at least in this context, is that in the first phrase "willingly" means of one's own free will as the opposite of being forced or compelled; whereas in the second phrase "eagerly" means doing so "from a real eagerness to serve" rather than from a desire for pay: "with enthusiasm" (Selwyn 230). If one serves as pastor out of a desire for monetary reward, it will be "shameful" greed for sure! "The proper attitude of an elder is an eagerness to give, not a desire to get" (Jobes 305).

IMPLICATIONS FOR PRACTICAL APPLICATION

As noted in chapter one, in Acts 20:28 Paul says to the Ephesian elders, "Therefore take heed to yourselves and to all the flock, among which the Holy Spirit has made you overseers." Surely the last clause refers to God's role, whether in the individual's sense of calling or through the church's recognition of God's will in the matter—or, as I believe, by both of these.

Indeed, the book of Acts offers some instructive, if limited, accounts of the Spirit's way of working in setting apart persons for ministry or leading them in doing ministry. One intriguing example is found in Acts 13:1-4, which refers to God's call for Barnabas and Paul to leave Antioch for what we have come to know as Paul's first missionary journey. The interplay is interesting. Verse 3 indicates that the church "sent" them, though the verb (Greek *apoluo*) inclines more to the meaning that they "released" them. Verse 4 indicates, correlatively, that the Holy Spirit "sent" them. Both were true, of course, and verse 2 provides the context: the Holy Spirit prompted the church[19] to set the two men apart for the work to which he had called them. One notes that the call was already extant[20] before the

---

[19] This was probably by means of a prophetic revelation; v. 1 may lay the groundwork for this by noting that there were active prophets and teachers in the church. These days, in my view, we do not have access to such prophetic revelations.

[20] "I have called" is perfect tense in Greek, focusing on an existing state of being.

church took action. It at least existed in the will of God, but I think it is almost certain that the Spirit of God had prompted Barnabas and Paul in this direction, and that their sense of calling was what led to the prayer meeting and the prophetic word.

Another example of the Spirit's leadership for ministry is found in Acts 16:6-10. Indeed, in this passage there is both negative and positive leadership. The Spirit of God first does not permit Paul and Silas to minister in Asian Ephesus (where they had apparently planned to go) or in Bithynia.[21] Then came a vision in the night, a man of Macedonia appealing for help. In response, Paul and his team concluded that God had called them to evangelize Macedonia. In this case, of course, the church was apparently not involved at all.

Granted, these incidents involved leadership for specific times and places of ministry rather than being called to pastor.[22] And they apparently included supernatural workings that were characteristic of the apostles during the transitional period in Acts when the biblical revelation was not complete. Even so, the principles illustrated may well parallel the pastor's calling. Regardless, the pastoral ministry is serious business, resulting, on the one hand, from the sobering call of God heard in the inner recesses of the soul and producing an eager desire for the work.

Even so, there is an "on the other hand": it is the church's responsibility to measure the man, to evaluate him to see if what he thinks is a call is validated in his life, character, and ability. This is

---

[21] This, too, was probably by means of prophetic revelation, either to Paul or to Silas.

[22] Similar experiences are found in Acts 8:29 when the Holy Spirit prompted Philip to approach the Ethiopian eunuch; and in Acts 10:19, 20 (compare 11:12) when the Spirit instructed Peter to go with the messengers sent by Cornelius.

clearly indicated in 1 Timothy 3, as well as in Titus 1, by the lengthy list of qualifications set forth, to be discussed in the next two chapters. The church does not simply seek to determine the genuineness and strength of the candidate's *desire* and sense of calling; indeed, Paul does not suggest an examination of the man's desire at all. Instead, the church looks carefully at the qualifications of the man; it weighs the evidence that can be objectively evaluated, all the while carefully seeking the leadership of God (Acts 14:23), and confirms by issuing its own call. Martin Luther gave little if any credence to a man's inner promptings but was of the opinion that the church alone issues the call to a pastoral ministry, that the Christian congregation serves to "make a preacher by its call alone" (39.313). In this he might have been more one-sided than necessary, but he was right to say (39.309) that "we must act according to the Scripture and call and institute from among ourselves those who are found to be qualified and whom God has enlightened with reason and endowed with gifts to do so."[23]

A man may well stand and say, "God called me to preach," and seem ever so sincere and well-meaning. But that is not enough on which to build the ministry of a pastor. Ordaining councils must take heed: it is not their job merely to judge the candidate's sincerity, but to measure the man in light of the biblical qualifications. Local churches must likewise take heed: it is not enough that a man have a good personality or an entertaining delivery, or be a good administrator; it is certainly not enough that an ordaining council

---

[23] The piece from which this comes (see the Bibliography) makes clear that Luther understood the right to call a pastor to reside in the church/congregation as a whole and not in any other person(s) or body.

decided to ordain him. The church must evaluate how well the man demonstrates not just the desire, but, even more important, the character, ability, and reputation that are represented in these passages.

In an ancient Christian writing known as *The Didache* (XI.3-9) the now unknown author instructs how to recognize whether an itinerant teacher is to be accepted or rejected: if he lodges with them three days (rather than one or two), or orders a meal when apparently speaking in the spirit, or if he asks for money, he is to be judged as a false prophet (*AF* 1.327). Perhaps this is "tongue-in-cheek" instruction; surely it was not meant to nullify the need for a pastor to be supported by the church. But the question of motivation is equally appropriate for all who are in any form of Christian ministry. John Wesley observed (10.494) that he did not blame a minister for accepting a yearly salary, "but," he said, "I blame his seeking it."

Is the man called by God? Let him show a sincere *desire* that has been planted and nurtured in his heart by the Spirit of God. Let him demonstrate the *motives* that the Lord commends: a willing, self-giving heart and an eagerness to serve regardless of the pay. And let the church issue its own call and set him aside for the pastoral ministry only after carefully seeking and finding in him the *qualifications* of character, ability, experience, and reputation that the inspired Paul gave to Timothy and Titus.

CHAPTER 3

THE PASTOR'S QUALIFICATIONS, PART ONE: WHAT HE MUST BE

1 Timothy 3:2-5, 7: "A bishop then must be blameless, the husband of one wife, temperate, sober-minded, of good behavior, hospitable, able to teach; not given to wine, not violent, not greedy for money; but gentle, not quarrelsome, not covetous; one who rules his own house well, having his children in submission with all reverence (for if a man does not know how to rule his own house, how will he take care of the church of God?); . . . Moreover he must have a good testimony among those who are outside, lest he fall into reproach and the snare of the devil."

Titus 1:6-9: ". . . if a man is blameless, the husband of one wife, having faithful children not accused of dissipation or insubordination. For a bishop must be blameless, as a steward of God; not self-willed, not quick-tempered, not given to wine, not violent, not greedy for money, but hospitable, a lover of what is good, sober-minded, just, holy, self-controlled, holding fast the faithful word as he has been taught, that he may be able, by sound doctrine, both to exhort and convict those who contradict."

The main emphasis of 1 Timothy 3:1-7 and Titus 1:5-9 is on the qualifications required of one who aspires to the pastorate. "The author's concern is with the kind of people to be appointed rather than with a job-description" (Marshall 472). "The main object of these is—not to enter into particulars—that [the pastors] should be of such virtue, so simple and modest, and in a word, so heavenly, that the gospel should make its way, no less by their character than by their preaching" (Gregory Nazianzen, *NPNF2* 7.219, *CSB*).

In the previous chapter I observed that the pastor's "call" is two-sided. His God-given desire (1 Tim. 3:1) focuses on the subjective side, the inner call. But that is not enough, and in both passages Paul devotes most of his discussion to the qualifications for a pastor. When we examine these, we are looking at the more objective perspective of the church, which has the responsibility to evaluate whether the man meets the requirements for the office and thus to determine by the evidence that God's call for him, indeed, is to a pastoral ministry. Based on these qualifications, under the leadership of God's Spirit, the church issues its own "call" of a man to a pastorate. "The will of the Lord concerning pastors is made known through the prayerful judgment of His Church" (Spurgeon 34, *CSB*).

Along with some others, Fee (78-79) represents these qualifications as not "distinctively Christian" but matching the qualities held in high esteem in the Hellenistic moral philosophy of the New Testament period. In other words, as verse 7 concludes, the pastoral candidate must not only have Christian virtues—which according to Fee, Paul assumes will be understood—but must "reflect the highest ideals of the culture as well." He may be right up to a point; it is true that even the non-Christian world often upholds noble virtues. But I think Fee overlooks that every virtue, regardless how grasped in the unbelieving community, becomes what it is truly meant to be only as a fruit of genuinely Christian faith.[24] We ought to read these, then, in the light of biblical understanding.

Most of the qualifications discussed in these two chapters are required of all Christians and not only of candidates for a pastoral ministry.[25] It is beyond my purpose to develop the implications of this. Obviously the pastor is rightly expected to manifest fully the character of a Christian. As Lenski (579-80) notes, we can bear with some faults in the congregation that cannot be tolerated for the pastor, since the pastor must set an example for (1 Pet. 5:3) and teach others. Marshall (472) appropriately notes that "there is no 'higher standard' for church leaders, but it is expected that they will actually show the qualities which are desirable for all believers." Liefeld (127) agrees that the passages provide "a standard of behavior that, while not different from that which all Christians should live by, is to be more rigorously monitored among elders and deacons."

There are sixteen qualifications listed in 1 Timothy 3 and twelve in Titus 1, though some overlap. Each is important and contributes to the total picture. No doubt there is more than one way to group them. In this chapter I will deal with the positive qualifications, the things a pastor *must* be. There are ten of these in 1 Timothy and ten in Titus, though some appear in both lists. In the next chapter I will deal with the *negative* qualifications.

---

[24] For a similar perspective, see Marshall (184).

[25] Being "able to teach" and not being novices are exceptions.

1. *Blameless*, in 1 Timothy 3:2, is literally not blameworthy or blameable: *anepilēmptos*, which etymologically implies that there is nothing to be held against the person, nothing in the man's life that people can take hold of to use against him. It means, in short, to be irreproachable in conduct and character. Chrysostom observed, "His life should be unspotted, so that all should look up to him, and make his life the model of their own" (*NPNF1* 13.438).

This could be included as one of the negative qualifications to be treated in the next chapter. But its overall impact is positive; any number of interpreters emphasize, appropriately, that this qualification stands over the whole list as a sort of summary of them all. Most of the rest of the qualifications, both positive and negative, expand on this as "the general basic requirement . . . for which the remaining qualifications . . . will provide concrete definition" (Marshall 477).

The word appears only in this epistle in the New Testament: in 5:7 of the widows that were to be approved for the church's support and of Timothy himself in 6:14. The lexical sources suggest that it means "above criticism, beyond reproach" (*LN* 1.436). In one sense, of course, no one is above criticism; but the qualified pastor conducts himself in a way that accusations against his character are unwarranted. In other words, the pastor's life does not give anyone valid excuses for rejecting his message or his leadership.

Blameless, in Titus 1:6, 7 is a slightly different word, *anenklētos*, though the two are close synonyms. This word describes "one who cannot be accused of anything wrong" (*LN* 1.438)—justly accused, that is. Marshall (154) may be right in suggesting it indicates that there is no (justified) accusation that is actually lodged against him. Calvin (21.2.291) gives as his opinion that Paul does not mean one who is perfect, "(for no such person could at any time be found,) but one who is marked by no disgrace that would lessen his authority. He means, therefore, that he shall be a man of unblemished reputation" (*CSB*).

Titus's word occurs three other times in the New Testament: in 1 Corinthians 1:8, Colossians 1:22 ("irreproachable"; KJV, "unreprovable"), and 1 Timothy 3:10. The last urges this as a qualification for the deacons; the first two speak of the Christians' standing without blame before God at the Second Coming.

This qualification must be important, in that it is stated twice in Titus, first for "elders" in general (v. 6) and then for the "bishop" (v. 7).[26] In verse 6 it is stated absolutely; in verse 7 an explanatory comment is added: "as the steward of God." This qualifying phrase may be taken in either of two slightly different ways. It may indicate the area where the blamelessness is to be found: namely, in his divinely-given stewardship. This would mean that he must be blameless in exercising his stewardship responsibilities. Or it may be a simile to suggest a comparison: just as any steward must give account and needs to be judged blameless, so the pastor—as God's steward—will want to be found blameless when giving account to his Master. The two ways of reading the words are not all that different: either way, the pastor is definitely charged by God with stewardship responsibilities and must carry out those responsibilities in such a way as to be blameless.

---

[26] The two words are frequently viewed as referring to the same office here, though some interpreters disagree.

A *steward (oikonomos)* is, as always in Scripture, one — typically, a servant — who has assigned responsibility to manage the affairs of another person. As such, he is accountable to his master and will be judged accordingly. It could be, then, that verse 7 looks to the future, when the pastor will give account before God whose steward he is. That will certainly be required, and a pastor must be conscious of this throughout his ministry. But since Titus is being charged to ordain qualified men as elders, it seems more likely that this qualification of blamelessness deals with his presently observable character, as does the similar one in 1 Timothy 3. Because the pastor's ministry is a stewardship from God, anyone set apart for that work must be one whose character and conduct, in general, are unassailable. Furthermore, a steward is a representative of his master and "the representative of God must be worthy of his master by having the kind of moral character which is worthy of him and which commends rather than condemns him" (Marshall 160).

2. *Husband of one wife* is, literally, "a man of one woman" or "husband of one wife": *mias gunaikos andra*. Precisely the same words appear in both 1 Timothy 3:2 and Titus 1:6.[27] There are, of course, arguments about the precise practical implications of this, especially as they relate to divorce and remarriage. Some interpreters think it rules out polygamy; it does that, of course, but the question is whether that is *all* it eliminates. More likely, it disqualifies a man who has been divorced and remarried. Indeed, a few interpreters

---

[27] The reverse phrase, "a woman of one man," appears in 1 Tim. 5:9.

would also rule out a man who has been widowed and remarried, since even he has not always had just one woman as wife.[28]

Does this mean that divorce and remarriage are *never* permitted for a Christian? There are differences of opinion as to what the Bible says about that, too, and this is not the place to explore that issue. Perhaps it is enough to say, here, that even if the Bible does permit divorce and remarriage in some exceptional cases (perhaps for sexual infidelity or desertion), it may still be the case that a pastoral candidate is not permitted such exceptions. Thieleke (176-77) urges that "in every case—including cases where the minister is declared 'innocent' in civil law—it is obvious that the minister [who remarries] must give up his office and should be urged to do so." Inaccordance with this view, many churches and denominations—including those in my tradition—will not ordain a man in such circumstances, taking this qualification to indicate (along with vv. 4, 5 below) that divorce and remarriage will hinder a pastor from the fulfillment of his duties as the leader he must be. In this, as in many other matters, the church has the right to determine the best way to apply the principles of Scripture.[29]

Regardless, every person who takes seriously this requirement will agree that the pastoral candidate, though not necessarily a married man, must if he is married be entirely faithful to his wife. Though he might well mean more, Paul certainly cannot mean less than that. A pastor's unconditional commitment to the one woman

---

[28] For a brief but helpful discussion of five views of this requirement, see Kent (122-26).

[29] Thielicke adds, "To hear the words '. . . till death us do part' spoken as a vow by one who himself could not or did not satisfy that obligation can provoke offense and seriously increase the already threatening danger that the church's blessing [on marriage] will be misunderstood as a mere conventional ceremony."

he has married, followed by uncompromising faithfulness to her alone, is essential to his ministry both before God and in the eyes of the congregation he leads. Both outwardly and inwardly, in deed and in thought, he must be a "one-woman man"—not just in legal marital status but in the commitment of his heart. In the secret recesses of his mind he does not fantasize about other women. He does not indulge in pornographic literature in print or on his computer!

3. *Temperate* (1 Tim. 3:2—KJV, *vigilant*) is *nēphalios*.

4. *Sober-minded* (1 Tim. 3:2; Tit. 1:8) is *sōphrōn*.

These two words are close synonyms, and the English translations often use one or more of the same words for them. They are not easy to distinguish, either in the translations or in actual meaning.

Nēphalios appears three times in the New Testament, translated in the KJV as *vigilant* (here) or *sober* (1 Tim. 3:11, of deacons' wives; Tit. 2:2, of older Christian men); the NIV always renders it *temperate*. There is a verb with the same root, *nēphō*, which apparently means to be "sober" in a figurative sense, on the analogy of one who is literally not drunk: "to behave with restraint and moderation, thus not permitting excess—'to be self-controlled, to be restrained, to be moderate in one's behavior, to be sober'" (*LN* 1.752).[30] Kent (126) takes it to mean being "spiritually sober, temperate, calm, and sober in judgment." Similarly, Fee (81) comments that it "is probably used figuratively to mean 'free from every form of excess, passion, or rashness' (cf. 2 Tim. 4:5)." Marshall

---

[30] The verb occurs in 1 Thess. 5:6, 8; 2 Tim. 4:5; 1 Pet. 1:13; 4:7.

(187) may be correct in combining the literal and metaphorical meanings: "freedom from dissipation and stupor which goes (for example) with abstinence from alcohol and keeps the person alert and active for the service of God."

Sōphrōn is used four times in the New Testament, variously translated in the KJV as *sober* (in these two lists), *temperate* (Tit. 2:2), and *discreet* (Tit. 2:5); the NIV renders all four by *self-controlled*. The fundamental meaning of the Greek stem is, apparently, to be of sound mind or "behave in a sensible manner" (*LN* 1.753). It refers, then, to a person who is sensible or moderate in his behavior. Kent (126-27) is right enough, though perhaps too limited, when he suggests that it means one who is serious or earnest, who has "the balanced judgment to relegate fun to its proper place" and is not a clown. Better to say that the word "depicts a balanced demeanor characterized by self-control, prudence and good judgment" (Marshall 184).

Together the two words picture a person who exercises sober control over himself in practice and thought, one who is self-disciplined and sensible, exercising sound judgment in his words and ways. His sound mind rules his behavior. A person who is "temperate and sober-minded" keeps himself under control and does not give up that control to unruled emotions, much less to drink or drugs.

This person is indeed the opposite of several of the negative qualities listed in the same passages, including being given to wine, greedy for money, violent, and quarrelsome; see the following chapter. Many a pastor has fallen, and spiritually blighted his church, as a result of various indulgences, whether in alcohol, drugs, or sex.

Only a man who has proved himself victorious in such matters is fit to be a pastor.

5. *Of good behavior* (1 Tim. 3:2) is *kosmios*, which is kin to *kosmos* ("cosmos"), the noun that often means our *world*. But the meaning of *kosmios* takes off from the fact that the *kosmos* is orderly or attractive; the related verb *kosmeō*[31] means to beautify. Thus the word used here describes one who is "well-ordered, moderate, becoming" (*LN* 1.748) and so one who conducts himself in a respectable, honorable way. The word suggests that which is both orderly and decorous and thus appealing to others: "a life which is well-ordered, the expression of a well-ordered mind" (Kent 127). Thus Knight (159), citing evidence from Moulton and Milligan, observes that the word was used "to describe a person as 'orderly,' 'well-behaved,' or 'virtuous,' which is the sense that it bears here: that which causes a person to be regarded as 'respectable' by others."

The word appears again in the New Testament only in 1 Timothy 2:9 where Paul urges Christian woman to wear "*modest* apparel." Some interpret that to mean clothing that is appropriate or suitable, rather than moderate or orderly. Either way, the meaning is similar. Here in 1 Timothy, as a description of a pastor's qualifications, it means modest behavior, behavior that doesn't attract the wrong kind of attention but strikes others as appropriate, orderly, appealing—and so respectable and honorable.

---

[31] The source of our "cosmetic."

6. *Hospitable* (1 Tim. 3:2; Tit. 1:8) is *philoxenos*, which etymologically means loving strangers but obviously in usage identifies what we call being hospitable, particularly where strangers are involved. The word appears just one other time in the New Testament in 1 Peter 4:9 where all of us are urged, "Be *hospitable* to one another without grumbling."

When the New Testament was written, the Christians in any community were often called on to provide lodging for other believers traveling among them, and the pastor would typically take the lead in this. In our affluent lives, with convenient motels and automobiles, not to mention airlines, we may sometimes wonder how to apply this quality. At the least, the pastor, like all Christians, should be quick to reach out and provide for people who are different, who are not of "our group" and are unlike us. Hebrews 13:2 speaks directly to this quality and still applies: "Do not forget to entertain strangers: for by so *doing* some have unwittingly entertained angels." Especially we must realize, and act accordingly, that the body of Christ is broader than our narrow interests.

7. *Able to teach*, in 1 Timothy 3:2, is paralleled in Titus 1:9 by the expanded words, "holding fast the faithful word as he has been taught, that he may be able, by sound doctrine, both to exhort and convict those who contradict." Though this is certainly a positive qualification, it deals not so much with the pastor's character as with his ability. It seems more appropriate, therefore, to treat this as definitive of the pastor's *role*. For that reason, I will treat these two passages in chapter five when focusing on the pastor as teacher.

In brief, the word is *didaktikos* and means *able to teach, skilled as a teacher*; it occurs only once more in the New Testament, in 2 Timothy 2:24, where a "servant of the Lord" must be *able to teach.* One manifestation of a man's call to pastor, recognizable by the church that must confirm that call, is a basic skill in communicating effectively the meaning of the Word of God.

One part of the wording in Titus, however, belongs to this chapter: "holding fast the faithful word as he has been taught." This focuses on the man himself. That the word he was taught is "faithful" means that it is entirely trustworthy and dependable.[32] The pastor must be unconditionally committed to rely on, to put his whole trust in, the Word of God that has been committed to him. The Bible is not simply something he teaches to others, but is first of all the foundation for his own life. Mounce (391) is correct in commenting that this "adds a theological dimension to a predominantly moral list" of qualifications.

8. *Gentle* (1 Tim. 3:3; KJV, *patient*) is *epieikēs*, which means something like "yielding, gentle, forbearing," showing the grace that we sometimes call clemency. It is not one of the two common words for "patience" in the New Testament but occurs just five times. It represents a quality that is the opposite of harshness in dealing with others, including especially those over whom one has some authority. It includes "the ideas of

---

[32] Compare Paul's frequent reference to a "faithful saying" in the Pastorals: 1 Tim. 1:15; 3:1; 4:9; 2 Tim. 2:11; Tit. 3:8.

patience, forbearance, and yielding," requiring a "disposition" that "will avoid much contention" (Kent 128).

The other uses of the word are in Titus 3:2 ("gentle") where it is urged on all believers, along with "showing all meekness unto all men"; in 1 Peter 2:18 ("gentle"), of the fair-minded masters to whom servants are glad to be in subjection; in James 3:17 ("gentle"), of the way of life taught by the wisdom that comes down from above; and in Philippians 4:5, "Let your *gentleness* (KJV, *moderation*) be known to all men."

It is especially important for pastors to have this quality as they deal with those under their leadership in the church, or with those outside the church. This does not mean that they will be "soft" on sin, but it does mean they will not be harsh and demanding, insisting on their own rights; instead, they will deal with others in clemency, showing gentleness and forbearing.

9. *One who rules his own house well* (1 Tim. 3:4, 5). I will touch on this again in chapter seven, which deals with the pastor as leader. "Rules" is *proistamai*, which etymologically means to "stand before" and thus in actual usage means to lead, guide, or direct—though even then in the spirit of one responsible for, concerned about, and caring for those who are being led. Fee (82) notes that the word "carries the sense of either 'to rule, govern,' or 'to be concerned about, care for.'" He adds that the following words, "take care of the church of God,"[33] give a clue to its meaning here, so that the latter

---

[33] I will deal with this expression in chapter six, "The Pastor as Shepherd."

implies "both leadership (guidance) and caring concern. In the home and church neither has validity without the other."

Obviously, "house" is used in the sense of *household, family.* The qualification, then, is that a pastor must first have proved himself a capable leader at home. Paul asks the obvious question, showing parenthetically why this qualification is so important: if one has not shown, at home, that he is a successful, caring, providing leader, one who wins the respect of his own family, how can anyone expect him to be such a leader at church? The expected answer is obvious.

What does this entail? Paul does not tell us everything, but he points us in the right direction with some specific implications. In 1 Timothy 3:4 he urges that the successful leader will have his children "in submission with all reverence," and in the parallel Titus 1:6, "having faithful children not accused of dissipation or insubordination." Surely both passages refer to children who are still under age and in the home.

First, then, the pastor's children will be "in submission"; the word is *hupotagē,* which literally means "placement under" and indicates submission, subjection, subordination, or even obedience. This noun and its companion verb (*hupotassō*) are used several times in the New Testament for submission to those in a position of leadership or responsibility: of citizens to their governing officials (Rom. 13:1), of wives to their husbands (Col. 3:18), of slaves to their masters (1 Pet. 2:18), and, as here, of children to their parents. Indeed, Ephesians 5:21 appears to mean that all believers are to be in subjection to all other believers!

Interpreters differ as to whether the "reverence" (KJV, "gravity") referred to in 1 Timothy 3:4 is meant for the man, indicating how he "rules" at home, or for his children as a complement to their submissiveness. I take it to refer to the man himself, and so it becomes, indirectly, yet another qualification. The word is *semnotēs*, meaning "behavior which is befitting, implying a measure of dignity leading to respect—'propriety, befitting behavior'" (*LN* 1.747). Marshall (189) defines it as "serious, dignified behaviour that is worthy of respect" and adds that people with this quality "take life seriously and devoutly and do not trifle." It may therefore be manifested at times in reverence toward God, or at other times in respectfulness toward others.

This is a man, then, who leads his family with seriousness of mind, respecting God and man, as well as his children, and therefore wins their respect and submissive following. Knight (161) observes, appropriately, that the children's submissiveness is reflective of "the character of their father's leadership." Chrysostom asks, pointedly, "For he who cannot be the instructor of his own children, how should he be the Teacher of others? If he cannot keep in order those whom . . . he has brought up, and over whom he had power both by the laws, and by nature, how will he be able to benefit those without?" (*NPNF1* 13.524).

The phrase used in Titus 1:6 fleshes out the way the children's subjection will be demonstrated. The most important word is *faithful* (*pistos*), which can be taken in either of two ways. Some regard it here as meaning "trustworthy or dependable": that is, one in whom confidence can be placed. Others take it in its more fundamental sense as *believing*: one who is a believer. The lexicons give both meanings, and both are found in the New Testament.[34] Either meaning would be appropriate here; my inclination is to the first, since it appears to go better with the submissiveness mentioned in 1 Timothy and with the rest of what is said in Titus.

Indeed, the rest of the phrase tells how their dependability (and submissiveness) will be practically demonstrated: they cannot rightly be accused of "dissipation" (KJV, "riot") or of "insubordination" (KJV, "unruly"). The first of these two words is *asōtia*, "behavior which shows lack of concern or thought for the consequences of an action — 'senseless deeds, reckless deeds, recklessness'" (*LN* 1.753). This definition seems weaker than the traditional understanding that the word means "debauchery, dissipation, profligacy," which the King James translators rendered as "riot." The word occurs only twice more in the New Testament: in Ephesians 5:18 (KJV, "excess"), where it is associated with drunkenness; and in 1 Peter 4:4 (KJV, "riot"), associated with an indulgent lifestyle characteristic of unbelievers. The adverbial form of the word is translated "prodigal living" (KJV, "riotous") in the parable of the lost son in Luke 15:13. Consequently, while either "recklessness" or "debauchery" will fit all these uses, the second seems better suited to each context; Luke 15:30 may well expound Luke 15:13.

"Insubordination" is *anupotaktos*, which originally means not being in subjection (as in Heb. 2:8) and as a result comes to mean "rebelliously disobedient" (*LN* 1.469), the meaning it obviously has

---

[34] The meaning "trustworthy" is confirmed in Mt. 25:21 and 2 Tim. 2:11, and the meaning "believing" in Gal. 3:9 and Jn. 20:27.

here, as well as in Titus 1:10 and 1 Timothy 1:9, the only other times it is used in the New Testament. It is therefore the exact opposite of the subjection required of the pastor's children in 1 Timothy 3:4.

Again, then, it is clear that the man who desires to be a pastor must first demonstrate successful leadership in his own home. As Knight (290) points out, this is nothing more than is asked of "every Christian father," but the pastoral candidate must demonstrate at least a characteristic success. A man whose children are reckless and self-indulgent, rebellious and disobedient—in short, not in subjection to their father and his instruction—is not likely to have the respect and influence needed to succeed in the pastor's role where he will attempt to lead a much larger number of people.

Liefeld (313) emphasizes that the pastor's children must not be guilty of the kind of behavior "that would bring public disrepute on the eldership and the church." That is certainly one of the things involved, though it is not the only thing.

In summary, the man qualified to be a pastor, if married, must be successful as a family man. His leadership at home should augur well for his effectiveness in leading the church. "The administrative ability required to cause a home to function smoothly will also be necessary if one is to superintend a church" (Kent 129). This includes his godly influence on his children. "The disposition of one's own children towards the apostolic faith reveals something about one's suitability to lead the church" (Marshall 480). Fee (173) notes that *anupotaktos*, the word translated "insubordination" (Tit. 1:6), is used of Eli's sons in the Greek Old Testament (1 Sam. 10:27); need it be said that Eli would not qualify as a pastor?

Does this mean that the pastor will *demand* his children's subjection? No doubt he will insist on it, but a subjection that is obtained *only* by force is never a true subjection. Any leader, even at home, who has to depend on exerting his authority to obtain a submissive following will soon fail. A successful leader *wins* respect by his own example and the wisdom of his leadership. Indeed, the very best commentary on this passage may well be the words in Ephesians 6:4 and Colossians 3:21; there we see precisely how the father is to bring about the condition described here.

10. Having *a good testimony among those who are outside* (1 Tim. 3:7) refers to the pastor's reputation among unbelievers, those outside the Christian family. "Testimony" (KJV, "report") is *marturia*, the word usually translated "witness or testimony." The effective pastor must have a good testimony within the unbelieving community around him; they watch the church and its pastor, often very critically, and *their response to the gospel depends on what they see.* "Leaders in particular are exposed to the public gaze and therefore must be all the more transparently upright in character" (Marshall 176). Lea (107) comments that "outsiders might not prefer his doctrines and morals, but they had to respect his integrity and commitment."

Does this mean that the man must always have manifested a good character, even before his conversion? No, this refers to the testimony of his life "since conversion" (Kent 130). Can a wicked man be saved, changed, and become a good pastor? Yes, but if a bad man becomes a Christian he must show the positive effects of his conversion long enough to win a good testimony from the unbelievers who know him well enough to speak on his behalf.

Paul provides a reason for the requirement: "lest he fall into reproach and the snare of the devil." "Reproach" (*oneidismos*) means having an insulting or disgraceful accusation lodged against one, and "snare" (*pagis*) is a trap, especially the kind used to trap birds. Here the trap is figurative, of course, and is set by the devil to catch those who minister for God. The disparaging accusation is shameful; it may be for a "real or imagined fault" and "implies scorn" (Spicq 2.585-86).

But what is the connection between this and the need for having a good testimony in the eyes of unbelievers? Evidently the meaning is that a pastor who does not have a good testimony in the unbelieving community will find himself the target of that community's insulting or derisive ridicule (whether accurate or not) and such occasions will be used by Satan to entrap and discredit the pastor. Knight (165) observes, "Either their making such an evaluation justly or his inappropriate reaction to an unjust evaluation will lead him to fall and to be caught in the snare of the devil." Ultimately, the situation may entail either the ruining of the pastor's reputation and ability to minister or his giving up in complete discouragement, or both. And we can be sure that the disparagement, and ensuing defeat, will extend not just to the pastor but to the church as well.

White (4.114) makes helpful observations on one aspect of this requirement. The church cannot afford, he says, to ignore the judgment of the surrounding world "in a superior spirit"; even unbelievers "have the law of God written in their hearts" (Rom. 2:15) and "up to a certain point, their moral instincts are sound."

11. *A lover of what is good* (Tit. 1:8) is just one word, *philagathos*, rendered as a lover of good men in the KJV. This is a combination of two Greek stems: the *phil-* means friend or lover, while *agathos* is the adjective for *good*. More likely, then, it refers to a person who loves *what* is good rather than good people—though of course a person who loves what is good will love others who are good.

Essentially all the lexicons, commentaries, and translations agree that "one who loves what is good" is the correct understanding. The good pastor will be "an ally and an advocate of everything worth while" (Kent 214). "An overseer's love for people is always to be correlated with a love for what God wants people to be" (Knight 292).

12. *Just* (Tit. 1:8) is *dikaios*, a word that occurs numerous times in the New Testament and is usually translated either "just" or "righteous," meanings that cannot be precisely distinguished from each other. As used here, it means one who is just in his dealings with others, treating them fairly and equitably and thus being in a right relationship with them.[35] Even so, Kent (215) is correct to remind us that God Himself is the one who finally and authoritatively pronounces this verdict on human conduct.

---

[35] Compare Mt. 1:19, where this adjective is attributed to Joseph, the (foster) father of Jesus.

13. *Holy* (Tit. 1:8) is *hosios*, rather than the usual word for "holy" (*hagios*, which has separatedness at the root of its meaning), though the two words are similar in meaning. Both can be applied to God as the only one who is absolutely described by either one. The word used here is sometimes applied to God, who alone is truly "holy" (Rev. 15:4). When applied to human beings, the word suggests "being dedicated or consecrated to the service of God—'devout, godly'" (*LN* 1.539), even *pious*. In 1 Timothy 2:8 it has that same sense: people who pray must lift up *holy* hands to God.

The pastor, then, must be a pious person, one who is devout and dedicated to the service of God. And it is clear that such a person will not just be consecrated to the cause of serving God but because of the nature of the God to whom he is consecrated will himself be of a holy character and conduct.

14. *Self-controlled* (Tit. 1:8; KJV, *temperate*) is *egkratēs*, literally suggesting the quality of one who holds himself in control and is therefore self-disciplined or self-controlled. This is the only time the adjective occurs in the New Testament, but its related noun (self-control) occurs three times (Gal. 5:23; Acts 24:25; 2 Pet. 1:6) and the verb (exercise self-control) twice (1 Cor. 7:9; 9:25). These passages instruct us in the practical meaning of the word.

Marshall (186), in defining the word, focuses on "self-control of the body and its desires," which is certainly involved. Perhaps a better way is to define this as the quality of one whose higher nature rules the lower nature. He imposes on himself the discipline that subjects lesser considerations to more important ones. It is this quality, for example, that causes the athlete to deny himself various freedoms and subject himself to rigid training because the end he seeks is worth the self-denial; compare 1 Corinthians 9:25. Chrysostom aptly observes that the word refers to "one who commands his passions, his tongue, his hands, his eyes" (*NPNF1* 13.525).

If a successful athlete will do this, how much more the pastor whose objectives are of such importance that the athlete's pale into inconsequence by comparison!

IMPLICATIONS FOR PRACTICAL APPLICATION

Though I will not pursue this in detail, some of these qualifications are of an "either-or" nature and some are "more or less"; indeed, some are both. One either is a capable teacher, for example, or he is not; but at the same time one may improve his ability and no two persons are likely to be equally capable. If the list were intended to require perfection, who of us could qualify? But there is surely a fundamental level at which each of these qualifications must be met for a man to qualify as a pastor. It is the church's responsibility to measure the man in light of these qualifications and thus to be assured that any man who claims to be called to preach ought to have a pastoral ministry.

Lest the discussion of qualifications focus too much on separate details, we ought to put the elements together into a unified picture. What sort of person is this candidate for the role of a pastor?

- Overall, he lives blamelessly, above reproach; his life does not give occasion for others to find fault or assail his character.

- He loves and seeks what is good, including the influence of good people.

- He is just in his dealings with others.

- He is dedicated to God and pious.

- He is faithful to the one woman to whom he has committed his life.

- He is self-disciplined and serious-minded.

- His conduct is orderly and appealing to God and man.

- He reaches out responsively to the needs of people, even strangers.

- He is skilled as a teacher of God's Word.

- He leads his family in such a way as to win their respect and the subjection of his children.

- He understands his ministry as pastor to be a stewardship given him by God.

- Even the unsaved bear witness to his integrity and character.

I will revisit this picture of the qualified pastor at the end of the next chapter, after examining the negative qualifications; this will include the question whether the list is unrealistic. But some things are already clear. The very first thing is a matter of what he is within himself—his own nature, in other words. The pastoral candidate must be a godly man, loving what is good, just, and holy, showing by his life that he is sensible and self disciplined: in short, of unassailable character. Only such a person will provide the church with sound, sensible leadership.

For another thing, the pastor ought first to demonstrate his pastoral ability *at home*. Although we cannot say that every pastor must be married, that will be typical; and often there will be children in the home. People must not expect a man to be successful in providing pastoral leadership for a church if he has failed to do so at home. If he has problems in leading his family—ranging from a demanding and dictatorial management style at one extreme to neglect of his wife or children at the other—he is likely to have the same problems in leading the church.

One more thing, here: the person qualified to be a pastor must be one who works with others in such a way as to win their following and respect—and this includes even those outside the church. In behavior he will be moderate and winsome, appealing to them. In his dealings with people he will be gracious rather than harsh and demanding. He will be hospitable and outgoing, reaching out to others in the name of Christ.

CHAPTER 4

THE PASTOR'S QUALIFICATIONS, PART TWO: WHAT HE MUST NOT BE

1 Timothy 3:2, 6: "A bishop then must . . . not [be] given to wine, not violent, not greedy for money, . . . not quarrelsome, not covetous, . . . not a novice, lest being puffed up with pride he fall into the same condemnation as the devil."

Titus 1:7: ". . . not self-willed, not quick-tempered, not given to wine, not violent, not greedy for money."

The previous chapter dealt with fourteen positive qualifications treated in 1 Timothy 3 and Titus 1. This chapter treats those that are negative: six in 1 Timothy and four in Titus; again, some of those given in Titus are either the very same words as those in 1 Timothy or close synonyms.

These negative qualifications—we may call them *dis*qualifications—tell what the pastor must *not* be; in each the negative is either included in the Greek word[36] or a "not" that stands in front of a

---

[36] Using what is called the alpha-privative.

disqualifying characteristic. Each therefore also implies a positive qualification that is in contrast to the negative characteristics.

It may well be that at least one of the reasons Paul singles out these disqualifying traits is the fact that they "are those to which persons in such positions are tempted" (Gealy 528).

1. *Not given to wine* translates *mē paroinos*, which occurs in the New Testament only in these two lists (1 Tim. 3:3; Tit. 1:7). The lexicons define *paroinos* as describing "a person who habitually drinks too much and thus becomes a drunkard" (*LN* 1.773) or as one "*addicted to wine*" (*BDAG* 780).[37] In other words, Paul refers to a person who does not give up self-control to the control of alcoholic beverages; the meaning would apply equally, by the way, to being a drug addict. This qualification is the opposite of, and implied by, the positive qualifications "temperate, sober-minded, and self-controlled"; see the preceding chapter.

This is not the place for extended discussion of temperance issues, including whether *oinos*, in the New Testament, is always fermented wine or whether the Bible teaches total abstinence. Whatever the answer to such questions, there is no excuse for waffling on the subject. Many churches and denominations, including the denomination of which I am a part, have a historic and covenant commitment to total abstinence, based on the consistent warnings of the Scriptures. One sure way to avoid being addicted to alcoholic drink is to abstain entirely. The unblameable example that any Christian,

---

[37] The etymology of the word, with *para*, beside, added to *oinos*, wine, may support this meaning; it reminds us of Prov. 23:30 with its warning to those who "tarry" at the wine.

including the pastor, can set for others is complete avoidance of alcoholic beverages. We are far removed from the days and circumstances when drinking water might need purifying by a modicum of wine (as perhaps in 1 Tim. 5:23), and there is neither need nor excuse for imbibing. If one wishes to claim that the Bible permits moderate drinking, he should be reminded that the Bible's apparent approval of slavery, or of polygamy in the Old Testament, does not justify the practice of either. Both were finally condemned as a result of applying the *principles* of biblical teaching. I am satisfied that the same applies to the use of wine or other alcoholic drink.

2. *Not violent* (KJV, *no striker*) is *mē plēktēs*, which also appears in the New Testament only in these lists (1 Tim. 3:3; Tit. 1:7). Without the negative, *plēktēs* means "a person who is pugnacious and demanding—'bully, violent person'" (*LN* 1.757). It seems clear that this qualification rules out those who expect to "win by intimidation" or are domineering, and certainly those who resort to actual violence. The qualified pastor does "not practice browbeating people" (Lea 111). He does not lash out at others, neither with fists nor with words! Chrysostom, in his discussion of this qualification urges that the bishop must not deal in insult or be insolent, lest "he that is insulted becomes more impudent, and rather despises him that insults him. Nothing produces contempt more than insult" (*NPNF1* 13. 525). (See also the fourth negative qualification, below.)

3. *Not greedy for money* (KJV, *filthy lucre*) is *mē aischrokerdēs*, which means not "shamefully greedy for material gain or profit"

(*LN* 1.292), not "fond of dishonest gain" (*BDAG* 29). Some of the old Greek manuscripts do not include this phrase in 1 Timothy 3:3, and some editions of the Greek text and versions do not have it; but it appears for certain in Titus 1:7 and is certainly among the qualifications of the pastor.[38] Furthermore, the adverb form of the very same word appears in 1 Peter 5:2 in discussing the motives and manner of the pastor. With this, compare negative qualification five, below.

Marshall (162) includes within the province of this prohibition such ideas as teaching for profit, allowing financial compensation to become one's primary motivation, unfaithfulness in managing the church's finances, or engaging in discreditable or dishonest business. At the least, the word disqualifies those who seek gain for themselves by ways that are shameful, dishonest, or disgraceful. One essential part of the pastor's blamelessness is in the way he obtains gain, whether money or other possessions. Not many things will ruin a man's ministry more quickly than questionable financial dealings, and pastors are often involved, in one way or another, in handling the church's money. This must always be done with integrity.

4. *Not quarrelsome* (KJV, *not a brawler*), in 1 Timothy 3:3, is *amachos*, which means not given to fighting, strife, quarrelling, disputes: "not contentious, peaceful" (*LN* 1.496) or "peaceable" (*BDAG* 52). Such a person is a peacemaker, and "Blessed are the peacemakers!" (Mt. 5:9). In its only other appearance in the New Testament, Titus 3:2 applies to *all* believers.

---

[38] It also appears as a qualification for deacons in 1 Tim. 3:8.

Some people are always looking for a fight. The man qualified to be pastor avoids conflicts and promotes peace whenever possible, though not at the sacrifice of biblical principles. See also the second negative qualification, above.

5. *Not covetous* (1 Tim. 3:3) is *aphilarguros*. This is not the usual New Testament word for covetousness; instead, it means "not loving money."[39] Thus it means "not being desirous or greedy for money—'not loving wealth, one who does not love money'" (*LN* 1.301). The only other time this word appears in the New Testament is in Hebrews 13:5, where all Christians are urged: "Let your conduct be *without covetousness*, and be content with such things as you have." Compare negative qualification three, above.

The pastor, above all, cannot afford to forget that love for money (noun form of the adjective used here) is a root of all sorts of evils (1 Tim. 6:10). He must always remind himself that dissatisfaction with what one has is at the root distrust of and dissatisfaction with God Himself. Contentment is the solution to covetousness, and as Paul says, later in 1 Timothy, "Godliness with contentment is great gain" (1 Tim. 6:6). The pastor does well to recall the words of Luther (21.201-2):

> Whoever wants to do his duty as a preacher and perform his office faithfully must retain the freedom to tell the truth fearlessly, regardless of other people. He must denounce anyone that needs to be denounced—great or small, rich or poor or powerful, friend or foe. Greed refuses to do this, for

---

[39] Literally, "not loving silver."

it is afraid that if it offends the bigwigs or its good friends, it will be unable to find bread. So greed puts its whistle into its pocket and keeps quiet. (*CSB*)

6. *Not a novice* is *mē neophutos*, which appears in the New Testament only in 1 Timothy 3:6. *Neophutos* (the source of our English "neophyte") literally means "newly-planted," and so Paul rules out a new convert, one who is new in the faith. This is at least part of what is meant in 1 Timothy 5:22 when Timothy is warned not to "lay hands on," apparently to ordain, anyone too quickly.

Only to the last three of the qualifications in 1 Timothy (3:4-7) does Paul attach additional comments; this is one of those, and the rationale is "lest being puffed up with pride he fall into the *same* condemnation as the devil." "Being puffed up with pride" translates one verb, *tuphoomai*, an uncommon and strong word that originally meant to be crazed or demented and then came to be used figuratively of one who is insanely arrogant or extremely proud (*LN* 1.765). Another lexicon is more restrained, defining it to mean being puffed up or conceited (*BDAG* 1021); the result is the same. Marshall (482) seems on the right track when he observes that it "suggests infatuation and bedazzlement with the authority and power related to office and perhaps the function of teaching." The word appears only once more in the New Testament, in 1 Timothy 6:4, where it is translated "proud."[40]

---

[40] Some sources suggest that in 1 Tim. 6:4 it means, instead, being blinded or clouded in one's judgment or discernment.

The point seems obvious: a man who is put in the prominent position of pastor too soon after his conversion is at serious risk of getting what we call "the big head" and acting in such a way as to bring on himself the same kind of condemnation or judgment (Greek *krima*) that fell on the devil.[41] Chrysostom comments, "If before he had learnt to be under rule, he should be appointed one of the rulers, he would be puffed up" (*NPNF1* 13.439).

The qualified pastoral candidate, then, is someone who has matured enough to prove himself, both as a Christian and in the responsibilities of ministry. The very word *elder*, given attention in chapter one, inherently demands this. We may not be able to put a precise age on this or number of years as a Christian, but we must not put into the position of pastor a person who is untried. He must give evidence that he can be effective in the position before he is put in the position! Indeed, sometimes the passing of time shows that a person who made an apparently genuine profession of faith was not truly converted at all.

7. *Not self-willed* (Tit. 1:7). The pastor must not be *authadēs*, "arrogant as the result of self-will and stubbornness" (*LN* 1.764). The only other time the word is used in the New Testament is in 2 Peter 2:10, where it is linked with a presumptuous daring that is not afraid to speak evil of "dignitaries" (apparently referring to angelic powers). The word is the opposite of both humility and submissiveness: "the headstrong, stubborn man who demands his own way without regard for others" (Kent 214). Marshall (161) thinks of this

---

[41] This is one of the biblical passages that hint at the reasons behind Satan's fall.

as a "rude indifference to the feelings of others." Luther (29.23) offers
the suggestion that it "refers to that stern and haughty attitude which
looks at itself in the mirror and despises others" (*CSB*). Chrysostom
pointedly warns that "he who ought to rule men with their own con-
sent . . . if he so conduct himself as to do everything of his own will
. . . makes his presidency tyrannical rather than popular" (*NPNF1*
13.525).

8. *Not quick-tempered* (Tit. 1:7; KJV, *soon angry*): that is, not
orgilos, used only here in the New Testament and meaning "angry,
quick-tempered, given to anger" (*LN* 1.761). It appears to mean that
the pastor must not be a man who is either characterized by anger or
easily angered: the two usually go together. The person who does not
control his temper is most assuredly not self-controlled and so lacks
one of the required positive qualifications treated in chapter three.

IMPLICATIONS FOR PRACTICAL APPLICATION

"In short, the bishop's life is not to be dominated or controlled
by wine or money, nor may it be one of strife, but rather it must be
one of peace and gentleness" (Knight 160).

I have already mentioned the possibility that Paul selected these
particular negative qualifications for the very reason that spiritual
leaders are especially vulnerable to such disqualifying indulgences.
Many a pastor has been brought down by failures on these very
points. I am thinking as I write this, for example, of a very good man
who was qualified as a pastor in every way but one: give him long
enough and something in the church to set him off, and his ministry

there was done! He couldn't control his temper. Another man I know forfeited his ministry as a result of mishandling the church's money; this lack of integrity did him in. I knew at a little more distance one who let himself be overcome by the monster euphemistically known as "John Barleycorn." Similarly, one got hooked on drugs and blew his own money and that of others and finally ruined his reputation with his family, the church abroad, and his friends. Yet another of the pastors I've known resorted to physical violence once too often and lost his church. I also recall several who have at least split the churches under their charge by unfair and domineering assertion of self-will.

The only failing I know of that dooms more preachers than these is sexual immorality; I have known many whose ministry was lost to an illicit affair. "The preacher who ran off with the pianist" is more than an exaggerated stereotype.

These are the kinds of things that the evil one places in the path of the pastor to bring about his downfall. For that reason, the candidate for the pastorate must *first* demonstrate victory over drink, temper, sexual passion, tendencies to violence, avarice, carelessness in handling others' money, greed, and arrogance. No wonder Paul warned Timothy himself to "flee youthful lusts" (2 Tim. 2:22); all of these disqualifications fall within that category.[42] Certainly then, the pastor must have been a believer long enough to prove that he is a person of self-control and soundness of mind.

---

[42] In this appeal, the word *lusts* is *epithumia*, which can refer to any strong passions, good or bad. It is, in fact, the noun form of the verb *desires* in 1 Tim. 3:1.

Thus it is that the negatives lead directly back to the positives discussed in the previous chapter. And that brings us back to the overall picture presented by both sets of qualifications in the two passages. Add these, then, to the practical applications drawn at the end of the preceding chapter.

The list of qualifications, positive and negative, is at once comprehensive and imposing! It speaks of the pastor's *character*, what sort of person he is. It speaks of his *maturity*, his spiritual development. It speaks of his *ability*, especially as a leader who teaches the Word of God. It speaks of his *motivation*, which must not be for money or domination or pride. It speaks of his *relationships* and *reputation*, both within and outside the Christian family.

Is this too idealistic to be real? Too intimidating to be lived up to? Can such a candidate be found? Surely God's Word does not intend to set an impossible standard. He must intend for the church to find such a man: a person who is mature, who has been tried and has proved himself. One who is aboveboard in his behavior, pure in his motives, respected by his family, conducting himself with personal integrity and practicing self discipline in deed and thought. One to whom even the non-Christian community bears a positive witness. One who demonstrates a proven ability to teach the Word of God with understanding and discernment.

In short, the pastor must be one whom the church can "call" to its most important office of leadership in confidence.

CHAPTER 5

THE PASTOR AS TEACHER

Ephesians 4:11: "And He Himself gave some [to be] . . . pastors and teachers."

1 Timothy 3:2: "A bishop then must be . . . able to teach."

1 Timothy 5:17: "The elders who rule well . . . especially those who labor in the word and doctrine."

Titus 1:9: "That he may be able, by sound doctrine, both to exhort and to convict those who contradict."

Hebrews 13:7: "Remember those who rule over you, who have spoken the word of God to you, whose faith follow."

Nearly every passage that speaks to the pastor refers to his responsibility to teach the church the Word of God. That is his first duty, and one that cannot be taken for granted: "The primary task . . . of the Christian minister is the preaching of the Word of God" (Lloyd-Jones 19). People "don't want our views, opinions, advice or arguments. *Is there any word from the Lord? Tell us that, they* demand" (Stewart 21).

1. 1 TIMOTHY 3:1-7

In this, the longest passage on the subject of the pastorate in the New Testament, Paul lists the qualifications of the pastor, most of which have been examined in the two preceding chapters. In the whole list there is but one *ability* that the pastor must possess: "A bishop then must be . . . able to teach" (v. 2).

The KJV phrase "apt to teach" translates just one Greek word, *didaktikos*, which means "able to teach" (NKJV), "skilful in teaching" (*BDAG* 240). Though this is one of the *qualifications* of a pastor, it is even more a skill that the pastor must possess. Indeed, as the only skill mentioned in the passage it points directly to the pastor's primary responsibility as a teacher of the Word of God: "This is the chief gift in a bishop, who is elected principally for the sake of teaching; for the Church cannot be governed in any other way than by the word" (Calvin 21.2.295, *CSB*).

Like all aptitudes, the ability to teach is one that can be developed and improved. A pastor must be committed to being the very best teacher he is capable of being. And the church that calls a man to be its pastor ought, without neglecting the other qualifications, to give this ability foremost consideration.

2. ACTS 20:28; 1 PETER 5:2

Both of these passages urge the pastor to "shepherd" (KJV, "feed") those for whom he is responsible, and the congregation is referred to by analogy as God's *flock* of sheep. The verb *poimainō* refers, broadly, to all the responsibilities of the shepherd in providing for the flock. For further development of this, see the next chapter.

For any shepherd one basic part of his work is to find grazing for the sheep and keep them well fed. Thus the Christian shepherd, as an able *teacher*, feeds the flock of God from the revealed Word of God: "Man shall not live by bread alone; but man lives by every *word* that proceeds from the mouth of the Lord" (Deut. 8:3). The pastor's paramount duty is to teach the people of God the ways of God from the Word of God, aided by the enlightening Spirit of God. In doing this he provides them spiritual sustenance and nurture.

3. HEBREWS 13:7; 1 TIMOTHY 5:17

These passages also mention, more or less in passing, the pastor's role as a teacher. In Hebrews 13:7 the writer urges his readers to "remember those who rule over you [see chapter seven], who have spoken the word of God to you." Though the writer is addressing the church as a whole, his words refer to the ministry of its leaders, surely the "elders" of the church.[43] Those leaders' primary work is summarized as having spoken the Word of God. They taught the believers and so fed the flock.

In 1 Timothy 5:17 (as in 1 Thess. 5:12), Paul urges that the elders who "rule well" be regarded with a sense of worth by the church. Chrysostom cites John 10:11 as an example, where Jesus says that the good shepherd gives his life for his sheep; likewise, then, to rule well means that because of his concern for his "sheep," one never spares himself (*NPNF1* 13.460).

---

[43] "Elders" does not appear in Hebrews except in 11:2, where O.T. persons are meant. It is possible that Hebrews 13:7 refers to *former* leaders, already dead at the time of writing; many interpreters think so. But in both v. 17 and v. 24 the very same language refers to *present* leaders.

Paul urges giving "double honor" to those who rule well, possibly suggesting "double pay" (as in the GNB) but more likely meaning "'double honor,' the honor and respect due those in such positions as well as remuneration" (Fee 129).[44] At any rate, Paul says that this is "especially" (*malista*, "most of all") for those who "labor in the word and doctrine"; that is not the only possible understanding of this word, which might be rendered "specifically." The NIV renders this "preaching and teaching," an appealing understanding. These are, in other words, *teaching* elders, obviously at least including, if not limited to, the pastors of the congregations.

"Labor" is *kopiaō* (as in 1 Thess. 5:12; see chapter seven). The pastor works hard, often against resistance, and Paul qualifies it here as (literally) "in word and teaching." Again, then, the pastor's primary responsibility lies in teaching the Word of God.

4. EPHESIANS 4:11, 12

In chapter one we learned that Ephesians 4:11 lists "pastors and teachers" as one of four gifts given to the church by the risen, ascending, victorious Christ. The other three are apostles, prophets, and evangelists.[45] This is the lone use of "pastor" in the English New Testament, which means "shepherd."

It seems clear that "pastors" and "teachers" refer to the same persons.[46] In the English "some" appears before each of the four but not

---

[44] Verse 18 develops a further, practical implication of the respect they should be given.

[45] For other and longer lists of spiritual gifts in the N.T., see Romans 12 and 1 Corinthians 12.

[46] A few interpreters do not equate the terms. See the discussion in Hoehner (543-45), for example; he agrees with Daniel B. Wallace that the second term is broader than the first and that while all pastors are teachers, not all teachers are pastors. See also O'Brien (300).

again before "teachers." This precisely matches the Greek, where the correlative use of *men ... de ... de ... de* distinguishes the four different offices. Thus Ephesians 4:11 also emphasizes that the primary activity of the "pastor" (shepherd) is teaching. "Pastor" names the office by the analogy of the shepherd-flock relationship; "teacher" names it by the real-life work that occupies the man. "A pastor/teacher is to make feeding the sheep a top priority — as Christ three times charged Peter to do (John 21:15-17)" (Hughes 133).

Verse 12 clarifies the purpose of the pastor's teaching and so helps us understand the nature of that teaching: namely, it is (literally) "for the perfecting of the saints for [the] work of ministry, toward the building up of the body of Christ."

This gives, in fact, *two* purposes: the first is intermediate and the last is final. Taking the last first, and briefly, the ultimate purpose of the pastor (and of everyone else in the church, for that matter) is the building up (edification) of the church as the body of Christ.[47] Verses 13-16 speak dramatically to this. When all the believers work together as God means them to, like all the parts of a person's physical body — joints, muscles, sinews, and the like — the church edifies itself and increases (v. 16). This is "the final aim of Christ's 'giving' to the Church. . . . to achieve his goal of building-up his 'Body'" (Schnackenburg 183).[48]

The purpose of the pastor's ministry, then, is a means to that end: to "equip" (KJV, "perfect") the saints to do this work of ministering

---

[47] Building the body of Christ includes both winning converts to Christ (evangelism) and the spiritual nurture of those won (edification). O'Brien (305) speaks of these as "growth in size" and "development of the church as an organism from within." Both are equally essential to the life of the church.

[48] Schnackenburg takes all the phrases to refer to the work of the ministers rather than the laity.

to build up the body of Christ: "The exalted Messiah gives ministries of the word to equip God's people for work in his service so as to build his body" (O'Brien 305). The noun used here, *katartismos*, probably means "equipping" in this context, though it might mean "restoring, repairing" or even giving "training or discipline." While this is the only time the noun appears in the New Testament, the corresponding verb (*katartizō*) occurs several times, as in Matthew 4:21 ("*mending* their nets"), 1 Thessalonians 3:10 ("*perfect* what is lacking in your faith"), and Hebrews 11:3 ("the worlds were *framed* by the word of God"). The one thing that all of these instances have in common is the idea that something is made to be what it was designed to be or ought to be.

That is precisely what the work of the pastor (and other leaders, for that matter) is: to prepare believers to minister effectively by instructing and equipping them to that end. The comma in the King James seems to separate "saints" from "for the work of the ministry," letting us read this as though the pastor does two things: *he* equips believers and *he* does the work of the ministry. But that was probably not what the translators intended and is almost certainly not what the original intends. Instead, the saints—all the believers in the congregation—are to be well equipped, fashioned, made fit for ministering. And the pastor, as their leader, is responsible both to set the example and to equip them in this way, especially by his teaching, but also by his administration or guidance in the functioning of the church.[49]

---

[49] For a thorough discussion of ways of reading the relationship between the phrases involved here, see Hoehner (547-49). My understanding is essentially the same as the fourth way in his list, which he adopts.

The "ministry" indicated here is *diakonia*, which means rendering "assistance or help by performing certain duties, often of a humble or menial nature — 'to serve, to render service, to help'" (*LN* 1.460). The word appears in several New Testament contexts that give concrete examples of the types of service that may be meant: Matthew 20:28; Mark 1:31; Luke 10:40; Acts 6:1; 20:24; Romans 12:7. Though it is the source of our "deacon," that is not the meaning here or usually in the New Testament. In the sense used here, *every believer is called to the "ministry"*!

For the purpose of this study, then, it is enough to say that an important part of the responsibility of a pastor is to see to it that the members of his congregation are made fit to serve. "Those in pastoral roles prepare God's people for works of ministry" (Hughes 134). They do this by example, by organizing the affairs of the church to that end, and by working with individuals who need such equipping. Most of all, they *teach* to this end.

5. TITUS 1:9

In chapter three, discussing the positive qualifications of the pastor, this verse was mentioned. Since it deals specifically with the pastor's role as teacher, this seems the better place to treat it in detail.

"Holding fast the faithful word as he has been taught" (v. 9). Literally, the clause reads, "holding fast the faithful/trustworthy word according to the teaching/doctrine." To hold fast (*antechō*) something is to cling to or be devoted to it, even to take an interest in or pay attention to it. "Faithful" is the same word as in verse 6 in the

expression "faithful children"; see the discussion in chapter three. Paul is thinking of the formal teaching given to Christians—their "indoctrination" we may say—and regards it as trustworthy and dependable. The pastor, in return, is to give the Christian teaching his careful and devoted attention.

The rest of the verse gives the reason for this: "that he may be able, by sound doctrine, both to exhort and convict those who contradict," those who speak contrary to the truth. The fundamental point of this is the same as in 1 Timothy 3:2, "able to teach." "Doctrine" is, after all, *teaching*.[50] Marshall (166) summarizes the whole in saying that "the purpose is that the overseer should be 'able' in exhortation and 'sound' (accurate) in correction and rebuke of false teachers. This makes a reference to the doctrinally pure Christian message much more suitable."

Paul adds an important modifier to the teaching the pastor should be able to give: it must be *sound* teaching. The word is *hugiainō*, often used in the New Testament to refer to physical health. Here, of course, it refers to teaching that is *spiritually* healthy—sound, correct—and in this way promotes the hearer's spiritual well-being. It is interesting that this word (for spiritual soundness) is limited, in the New Testament, to the pastoral epistles but occurs there a number of times. "Sound doctrine," as here, appears again in 1 Timothy 1:10; 2 Timothy 4:3; and Titus 2:1. "Sound (wholesome) words," essentially the same as sound doctrine, occurs in 1 Timothy 6:3 and 2 Timothy 1:13. And "sound in the faith" is in Titus 1:13 and 2:2: only those who have had healthy teaching/doctrine will be healthy in the faith.

---

[50] "Doctrine" is from the Latin *doctrina*, "teaching," equivalent to the Greek *didaskalia*.

What will be the result of this ability in teaching? As translated in the NKJV (and the KJV), the "both . . . and" clause sounds like *one* effect: namely, "to exhort and convince," with both of these targeting "those who contradict" (KJV, "gainsayers"). But the word-order in the Greek is more likely *two* effects: literally, "that he may be able both to be exhorting in/by the healthy teaching and to be convincing the gainsayers." In other words, exhorting by sound doctrine is his broad responsibility and it includes all who will hear him, especially the church; then convincing those who contradict is the additional objective. "The pastor ought to have two voices: one, for gathering the sheep; and another, for warding off and driving away wolves and thieves" (Calvin 21.2.296, *CSB*).

"Exhort" is the very common Greek word *parakaleō*, used many times in the New Testament and variously translated as "beseech, appeal to, exhort, encourage, comfort," etc. In my view it has two slightly different focal points in different contexts, either *urging* or *encouraging*; the two ideas are closely related and often both are in view, as here. The pastor's "sound" teaching will encourage believers and urge them in the right application of the revealed will of God for them. It will also appeal to the erring, both within and without the church, to bring their lives into conformity with the will of God.

It will also aim to "convict those who contradict" the truth of God's Word and the gospel. "Convict" (KJV, "convince") is *elenchō*, which appears often in the New Testament and has various shades of meaning: bring to light, expose, convict, convince, reprove, correct. The fundamental idea is "to state that someone has done wrong, with

the implication that there is adequate proof of such wrongdoing—
'to rebuke, to reproach'" (*LN* 1.436). The word does not necessarily
imply that the rebuke is successful in bringing the wrongdoer to
change his way, but that is the objective. John the Baptist was not
successful in *rebuking* Herod concerning Herodias (Lk. 3:19), for
example. In 2 Timothy 3:16 Paul uses the noun form of this same
word when he writes that "All scripture is given by inspiration of
God, and is profitable for doctrine [teaching], for *reproof*. . . ." And
this obviously has the purpose of bringing about the kind of "correction" of one's ways that is indicated in the very next words in that
verse.

"Those who contradict" is *tous antilegontas*: literally, "the ones
speaking against." They are the ones who speak in opposition to the
truth of God, to the Christian way; they object and let it be known,
they resist the Christian teaching.[51] The pastor must at least expose
their error and rebuke their wrongheaded resistance, though he does
so in love (Eph. 4:15) and seriously attempts by teaching the Word
of God as capably as he can to convert the objector to faith. In some
circumstances, of course, this rebuke or refuting may have to involve active church discipline.

Obviously the following verses (10, 11) expand on these "gainsayers." Paul observes that there are many such objectors out there
"whose mouths must be stopped." To this end Paul says that Titus
himself should "rebuke" them sharply (v. 13), using the very same
word as in verse 9. Even that sharp rebuke, however, has as its goal

---

[51] Of course, in this epistle the reference may be to specific opponents of the Pauline mission and gospel
that Titus would have to face. Even so, what is said leads to the larger task of pastors in any place and
time.

"that they may be *sound* in the faith," picking up yet another important word from verse 9. My purpose here, however, does not include exegetical treatment of the rest of the chapter.

Chrysostom's comment is to the point: "He who knows not how to combat the adversaries, and to 'bring every thought into captivity to the obedience of Christ,' and to beat down reasonings, he who knows not what he ought to teach with regard to right doctrine, far from him be the Teacher's throne" (*NPNF1* 13.525). In the same passage Chrysostom observes that this requires "skill in the Scriptures" and that if a man has all the other qualifications but lacks this one he lacks what is necessary to be a teacher.

IMPLICATIONS FOR PRACTICAL APPLICATION

The divinely approved pastor must be one who effectively communicates the Word of God. This qualification describes what may be the single, most important part of his ministry. To be sure, there is much else a pastor must do in his work as shepherd of the flock. The following chapters will focus more on that. Day in and day out, however, he must give himself to the teaching of the Word to those entrusted to his pastoral care.

Snodgrass (214) makes the helpful point that "*language creates a community* . . . . Preaching is the opportunity every preacher has to bring order out of chaos on the basis of the Word of God." Furthermore, to the degree that the pastor's teaching is based on the authoritative and inspired Word of God—and *only* to that degree—he can teach with the authority of "Thus says the Lord." Hoehner (545) rightly distinguishes between the biblical *prophet* who spoke "under the *immediate* impulse and influence of the Holy Spirit," and the contemporary *pastor-teacher*, who gives "instruction on that which was already revealed."

When the church begins to consider the possibility that a given person may be called by God to a pastoral ministry, there ought to be manifested in him a basic aptitude for teaching. But this aptitude is more than a mere "either-or" kind of thing, and a natural gift is only a starting point. The ability to teach is one that can be developed, and a good pastor will focus on improving his skill in teaching throughout his ministry.

One pastor I know never enters his pulpit on Sunday without having first practiced his entire sermon out loud, often to his wife or a friend. Being a skillful teacher is worth enforcing that sort of discipline on oneself. Studying, writing, organizing, rewriting, "tasting" the words one will use—the orator's skill requires what one of my homiletics teachers used to call blood, sweat, and tears.

Preaching, of course, is the pastor's most formal medium for teaching, though it is not the only one.[52] In any event, the pastor's sermon should be a means of giving oral teaching regarding the Word of God and its practical implications. A sermon is in one sense an art form, and as such the preacher is justified in giving it the preparation and attention required to make it appealing and persuasive. But at last it is a tool for teaching the people of God how to apply the Word of God to their lives. Their spiritual well-being and maturity result from

---

[52] Indeed, there may be little real difference between a *sermon* and a *lesson*—though I often make the distinction about my own preaching and teaching, and I think we usually know what we mean by not equating the two. My purpose does not include pursuing the differences; see Forlines (6/80) for one view.

a proper diet of revealed truth, and the pastor's accountability will be measured in that light.

In the preceding paragraphs I have emphasized the formal, public teaching that the pastor gives his assembled congregation. But I hasten to add that the pastor ought also to teach the individuals under his watch-care. During some of my formative years, my first "real" pastor was a man who spent a large part of each week out in the community, visiting in the homes of the members (as well as of the unchurched) and giving personal attention to their spiritual needs.

I would recommend that every pastor read at least some parts of a little book entitled *The Reformed Pastor*, written by Richard Baxter in the mid-seventeenth century[53] and intended to be an exposition of Acts 20:28, one of the passages of prominence in my own work (see chapter six). In his chapter on "The Oversight of the Flock," Baxter begins by acknowledging the importance of "the public preaching of the Word." He says (78):

> It is a work that requires great skill and especially greater life and zeal than any of us can ever bring to it. For it is no small matter to stand up before a congregation and deliver a message of salvation or judgment as from the living God, doing so in the name of the Redeemer. It is no easy matter to speak so plainly that the ignorant may understand us. Or to preach so seriously that the deadest hearts may feel us. Or to reason so convincingly that those who are argumentative may be silenced.

---

[53] The original was, of course, not a "little book" at all; I refer to a more recent abridgement (in 150 pages) defined in the bibliography.

But Baxter's primary focus is on what he calls "personal ministry"; he said that "it is the unquestionable duty of all ministers of the Church to catechize and to teach personally all who are submitted to their care" (5). He practiced systematically visiting the homes of his parishioners, examining them spiritually, and giving individual instruction as needed, including going beyond a formal catechism he required of them. The description of these efforts (6) is convicting: "We spend Mondays and Tuesdays from morning to about nightfall, taking some fifteen or sixteen families each week in this work . . . . With two assistants, we make our way through all of the congregation—about eight hundred families—and teach each family during the year." He said (114), "I conclude, therefore, that public preaching is not enough. You may study long, but preach to little purpose, unless you also have a pastoral ministry."

Our circumstances are not entirely the same as Baxter's. But I am persuaded that the faithful shepherd of the flock will minister not just to the assembly but to the individual "sheep," for whose spiritual well-being he is responsible.

To be an Affective teacher of the Word, whether to the congregation as a whole or to individual believers, the preacher-teacher must first master the Word. No one teaches well who has not first studied well; the pastor must give himself to the continued, consistent, and careful study of the Bible, making use of all the tools at his disposal in order to be absolutely sure he understands exactly what God has said. We do honor to the fact that God has spoken when we labor carefully to determine the precise meaning of His words.

Snodgrass (225) is right to complain that "many pastors get involved in all sorts of other activities and do not develop their knowledge and ability to explain the Word." Hughes (134) speaks about pastors who begin preparation of their Sunday sermons on Saturday night while watching television, and then observes: "Many pastors have a two- or three-year barrel of sermons which they recycle—usually in succeeding churches." For shame! That kind of "study" does not equip the pastor as an able teacher of the Scriptures.

Ability in teaching includes insight into how to apply God's Word to life. God has not spoken to inform us of sterile truths and we do not study the Bible merely to unravel the knots. Instead, the Bible is intended to be lived, and it is the pastor's duty to help his people understand what its principles are and how to put them into practice.

CHAPTER 506

THE PASTOR AS SHEPHERD

Acts 20:28: "Take heed . . . to shepherd the church of God."

Ephesians 4:11: "And He Himself gave some [to be] . . . pastors and teachers."

1 Timothy 3:5: "How will he take care of the church of God?"

1 Peter 5:2, 3: "Shepherd the flock of God which is among you, serving as overseers . . . nor as being lords over those entrusted to you, but being examples to the flock."

In chapter one I pointed out that the word *pastor* means a shepherd and so looked at the office from the analogous perspective gained by viewing the church as God's flock over which He has assigned shepherds. Everything that the New Testament says about the office, then, refers in one way or another to the pastor's shepherding responsibilities.

This concept is, in fact, older than the New Testament community. The Old Testament often presented the idea that Israel was God's flock and its leaders under-shepherds. Even in the Qumran community represented in the Dead Sea Scrolls, of the overseer (*mebaqqer*) it was said that he "shall love them [the members of the Qumran community] as a father loves his children, and shall carry them in all their distress like a shepherd his sheep" (*CD* 13.7, cited in Hillyer 142).

Though as teacher (chapter five) and leader (chapter seven) the pastor is occupying the place of a shepherd, some of the things said about the pastor speak with special force to the fact that the pastor is the shepherd of the flock. Here I am especially interested in the implications of the word *bishop* or *overseer* and the verb translated "shepherd" (KJV, "feed") the flock.

1. ACTS 20:28-31

Toward the end of Paul's third missionary journey, he stopped briefly at Miletus[54] and summoned "the elders of the church" in Ephesus to meet him for what is often called a "farewell address" (see Acts 20:17, 38). The entire speech is instructive, and I am tempted to exegete all of it.[55] But most of it is a description of Paul's own personal ministry at Ephesus, earlier on the same journey. While it might therefore be applied to the ministry of a pastor—though of course Paul was not a "pastor" in a contemporary sense of the word—only verses 28-31 speak directly to the elders who responded to Paul's bidding. It is clear, then, that Paul's words to the elders are definitive for the work

---

[54] On the coast of the small Roman province of Asia.

[55] I have done this on another occasion: see the no longer published *Dimension*, 1:1 (summer, 1984), pp. 11-18.

of pastors.[56] As Stott (*Acts* 323) observes, the passage will help us "rehabilitate the noble word 'pastors,' who are shepherds of Christ's sheep, called to tend, feed, and protect them."

a. The pastor's people as God's "flock." Paul's first description of the church which the pastor serves is as a "flock" (*poimnion*), an analogy that is precisely appropriate for viewing the leader as a *shepherd* or "pastor" (*poimēn*). In both the Old and New Testaments the people of God are frequently identified as a flock of sheep.

I note, in passing, that Paul urges the elders to take heed to *all* the flock. It is possible that Paul means the universal church as God's whole flock, with each under-shepherd having his assigned portion of the church as his individual area of responsibility, as probably to be seen in 1 Peter 5 below. But it is at least as likely that Paul is referring to each pastor's congregation and means that the pastor must shepherd all those under his care. This much is true, regardless: none of the sheep should be neglected.[57]

Paul further identifies the flock as "the church of God." Church is *ekklesia*, literally "called out." In the New Testament world this word was used both by the Jews and the Greeks. The Jews found it in the Greek Old Testament (LXX) as a translation for the "congregation" of Israel (Acts 7:38). The Greeks used it, for example, for an "assembly" of citizens in a city. The word implies both privileged standing and active assembling.

---

[56] Not all speeches recorded in the Bible were divinely inspired; some were by ungodly men. But we are on safe grounds to assume that this one had the Lord's own authority behind it; it is apostolic, to be sure, and everything about it resounds perfectly with the rest of the N.T. teaching on the subject.

[57] This may well speak to the need for what Baxter called a "personal ministry," as mentioned in the concluding section of the previous chapter.

What is important, here, is that this is *God's* church, not the pastor's.[58] And this fact is reinforced by the added clause, "which He purchased with His own blood." *Purchased* is a simple aorist indicative (looking back at the whole redemptive act) of *peripoieomai*, which means to make one's own, "to acquire possession of something, with the probable component of considerable effort" (*LN* 1.565). In this instance, that effort is heroic indeed: "with His own blood." The order of these words differs slightly in various manuscripts: some say clearly "with his own blood" while others could be read this way or as "by the blood of his own," meaning "his own [Son]." For our purposes here this makes no difference: the church belongs to God, it is His flock, by virtue of the shed blood, the sacrificial, redemptive death, of the Lord Jesus, who is in fact God. Given that the church is God's own flock by such a costly purchase, no pastor dare usurp authority over it!

b. The pastor's role as an overseer to shepherd the flock. One phrase in verse 28 stands out in indicating both the role of the pastor and how he obtained it (literally): "among/in which the Holy Spirit placed you [as] bishops/overseers to be shepherding/tending the church of God." The role of the pastor, once again, is as an *episkopos*, an overseer or bishop; Boice (349) may be right in saying that "Paul is not using the word in an ecclesiastical sense to describe a certain order of clergy . . . . Rather he is speaking of all the elders of a local church as overseers, that is, as those who have a responsibility for the oversight of Christians in their area." Even so, this is precisely the role of a pastor.

---

[58] I heard of one pastor who for this reason refused to use the expression "my church"; instead, he referred to "the church I serve."

Indeed, the pastor is to be "shepherding" (*poimainō*) the congregation in his charge. These two words (*episkopos* and *poimainō*) are the same words that have already been discussed at some length in the treatments of other passages. I observe again that "feed" (in the KJV) is broad and encompasses all the duties of a spiritual shepherd to the spiritual sheep entrusted to his watch-care. "As a shepherd protects, cares for, and feeds the sheep, so through teaching and exhortation these presbyter-bishops are to nurture those in their charge" (Larkin 298). Forlines (2/80) comments, "The shepherd has a deep concern for the needs of his flock. He ministers to their needs. He protects them from danger. He leads them rather than drives them. It is a caring type of leadership."

How does the pastor come into such a place of responsibility? The answer is that the Holy Spirit has put him there. Though the King James says "*over* the which," the Greek simply says *among* or *in* which; the preposition is *en*. Obviously, the relative pronoun *which* refers to the noun "flock." The point is that God Himself, as the Holy Spirit, places the person as a pastor in the flock/church. While this does not discount the church's participation in calling a pastor, it traces the decision back to its ultimate source. As Williams (355) observes, these elders had (as in 14:23) been "formally appointed by the laying on of hands with prayer," but that ordination presupposed a "divine call," the active work of the Holy Spirit Himself.

c. The pastor's attitude: take heed. Like two bookends an important admonition is wrapped around this brief appeal to elders: "take heed" (v. 28) and "therefore watch" (v. 31). The former is *prosechō*, "to be in a continuous state of readiness to learn of any future danger, need, or error, and to respond appropriately — 'to pay attention to, to keep on the lookout for, to be alert for, to be on one's guard against'" (*LN* 1.333).[59] The latter is *grēgoreō*, which means to be awake, either literally or figuratively — here the latter: "to be in continuous readiness and alertness to learn — 'to be alert, to be watchful, to be vigilant'" (*LN* 1.333). The two words are close synonyms here, suggesting both deliberate focus and watchful guardianship.

The context for this focus and watchfulness is specific, and verses 29, 30 define: untrustworthy persons will arise to ravage the flock with error and create division. Staying with the analogy of sheep, Paul likens these dangerous pretenders to wolves that are "grievous" (KJV). This adjective, *barus*, literally means "heavy, weighty, burdensome, troublesome," and so for wolves as enemies of sheep it means "fierce," "savage." Translated into real life, these are false teachers who invade the flock for their own ends, to consume and destroy.

Verse 30 apparently translates the metaphor of verse 29 into real life. Men will arise and speak "perverse" things for the purpose of drawing others away from the faithful church after themselves. "Perverse" is *diastrephō*, which always, in one way or another, refers to that which is turned away from what it was or ought to be. The NIV renders "distort the truth," and that is the idea. These "wolves" speak twisted, distorted things in order to create their own following and thus ravage the church. It is the pastor's responsibility

---

[59] The verb can also mean "to give oneself to" something, which could be the meaning here, but the meaning quoted fits better in this context.

to be watchful and on guard, to recognize and expose error. This is one of the ways he exercises watch-care as shepherd over his flock. As overseer, the pastor's efforts are to ensure "that no one without and no one within would damage the flock for which Jesus died" (Boice 349).

In the rest of verse 31 Paul reminds the Ephesian elders of his own way of fulfilling that responsibility; for the nearly three years he had been with them he did not cease to warn everyone night and day and to do so with tears. In this he had set the example for the elders, and he expects them to do likewise. Thus the pastor's work specifically includes "warning" those in his charge. This verb is *noutheteō*, which etymologically means to "put in mind," and so can mean simply to instruct; but it often carries the notion of instructing for the purpose of correcting and even to warn of the consequences of wrongdoing: "the correction of the will that presupposes opposition" (Larkin 298). No doubt all these shades of meaning are wrapped up here in the pastor's instruction that is motivated by the dangers of false teaching that may "come in" (v. 29) or "rise up" (v. 30). The very same word appears in 1 Thessalonians 5:12-14. (See chapter seven.)

What is the meaning of "your own selves"? Does this suggest that the purveyors of false teaching will arise from among the elders themselves? Or is "your own selves" broader, looking to the whole believing fellowship? Probably the latter, although experience makes clear that erroneous teaching often comes from among those who have shepherding responsibilities. The faithful shepherd-pastor guards both himself and his flock from error by holding firmly to the Word of God in setting the course of his own thinking and in his teaching.

2. 1 PETER 5:1-4

Peter addresses these words directly to "the elders who are among you," which might be plural either because there were several churches involved (1:1) or because any given church had a plurality of elders. Either way, Peter's words are certainly addressed to pastors and the passage is clearly appropriate for this study.

Verses 2-4 contain Peter's words for the "elders." Paul's instructions to Timothy and Titus focused on qualifications that ought to be kept in mind when pastors are set apart for their work. Peter focuses, instead, on the work itself and how the pastor is to go about it, especially in vv. 2, 3.

a. The command in verse 2, to "shepherd the flock of God," is the major focal point of the whole passage; it is the only imperative verb and sums up the pastor's duties as a whole, using the analogy of the church as God's flock and the pastor as the shepherd.

As in Acts 20:28 (above), "shepherd" (KJV, "feed") is *poimainō*, a broad word that includes all the shepherd's responsibilities to the flock. It is helpful to translate it *shepherd* (NKJV, NASB)[60] or *tend* the flock of God. A good shepherd does many things for the sheep entrusted to his care: he guards them, he finds pasture for them and grazes them there, he leads them back and forth, he nurses them when hurt, and so on. In short, he *cares for, looks out for* the flock and works to meet all its needs.

Just so, the God-called and church-called pastor has one ministry: to meet the needs of the congregation with a spiritual shepherd's heart of care for them. To be sure, "feeding" them the Word of God,

---

[60] The NIV renders, "Be shepherds of God's flock," which is equally appropriate.

as an apt *teacher*, is a key part of his shepherding; see the previous chapter. But his responsibility does not end there; he must bind up their wounds, give them guidance, guard them from falsehood, and in every other way look out for their spiritual welfare.

   b. Side by side with the one commanding verb ("shepherd/ feed") is the participial phrase rendered "serving as overseers" (KJV, "taking the oversight thereof"). The purpose of this phrase is, apparently, to further clarify or define the shepherding ministry stated in "shepherd the flock." The shepherding *is*, in fact, carried out by exercising this oversight. Goppelt (343) appropriately renders, "Shepherd the flock of God among you by carrying out your service as overseers"; he points out, correctly, that both here and in Acts 20:28, the shepherding (*poimainō*) is explained by the exercising of oversight or watch-care (*episkopeō/episkopos*).[61]

The KJV translation, "taking the oversight," might be understood in the wrong way. It does not refer to a specific action at the point of decision and it does not imply that the pastor "takes" the position at his own initiative. The participle is *episcopeō*, the verb form of the noun translated "bishop" (as in 1 Tim. 3:1, 2; Tit. 1:7). And it is a present tense participle that views the action while it is in progress. A helpful translation would be "exercising oversight" or "serving as overseers" (NKJV, NIV): "exercising your pastoral care" (Selwyn 230).[62]

---

[61] Goppelt, here, thinks that a common tradition must be behind 1 Peter 5:2 and Acts 20:28; but that need be nothing more than a broad usage, in the early church—both Pauline and Petrine—of these terms to describe pastoral leadership.

[62] Some of the ancient manuscripts do not have this participle at all, as reflected in the NASB translation.

Together, these first two verbs ("shepherd/tend the flock, exercising oversight") lay down the subject Peter has in mind, indicating the nature of the elders' ministry. The rest of the passage is the most important part, describing just how they are to exercise that ministry.

c. Indicating the manner of the pastor's ministry are three "not this, but this" phrases that describe the way the pastor-shepherd is to go about his work.[63] The three phrases are: (1) "not by constraint but willingly"; (2) "not for dishonest gain but eagerly"; and (3) "nor as being lords over those entrusted to you, but being examples to the flock." The rendering of Jobes (304) is excellent:

1. Overseeing them not as if forced, but willingly, according to God
2. Overseeing them not as greedy for gain, but eager to be of service
3. Overseeing them not as domineering, but being role models for the flock.

The first two of these phrases deal with motives and were examined in chapter two as part of the discussion of the pastor's call. The third, however, fits well with our present discussion of the pastor as shepherd, given that it refers to the way the pastor relates to the congregation.

Negatively, the pastor does not "lord" it over the flock. "Being lords" is a verb, *katakurieuō*, and it means to "exercise lordship" or "exercise dominion." In simple terms, it means to have the place of a *kurios* (lord), to rule as a lord or master. From Peter's perspective,

---

[63] Grammatically, these phrases qualify the participle "exercising oversight"; but for all practical purposes they modify both of the preceding verbal forms.

then, the pastor is *not* a "lord" or "master" over the flock at all; much less does he exert his influence by being domineering or dictatorial.

This fits precisely with what Jesus said to the apostles in Matthew 20:25-27, and the parallel Mark 10:42-45 and Luke 22:25, 26, paraphrased: "Those ruling the nations *exercise lordship over* [*katakurieuō*, as here] them, but that is not to be the way for you; whoever wants to be great must be your servant [*doulos*, slave]." Goppelt (347) is on the mark to observe that "the 'domination' customary in the political realm" is therefore "the opposite of the principle of service that is to be in effect among the disciples." Indeed, in Luke 22:26, "he who governs" is the very same word— *hēgeomai*, to lead—that is used in Hebrews 13:7, 17, 24 for those who "rule" over the church (see further chapter seven), and there Jesus requires that they lead by serving.

In the KJV wording, "God's heritage," *God's* has been supplied. "Heritage" is, simply, *tōn klērōn*, which means something like the portions assigned by lot. This is not the word that typically means inheritance or heritage. Instead, it is originally (in the singular) the word for a "lot" that is cast, and it came to mean a portion or share assigned by lot—though the idea of the lot-casting grows dim in some contexts, as here. At any rate, the NKJV appears to catch the right idea: "those entrusted to you."

One question, here, is why the word is plural (in Greek). Some think it suggests "the various parts of the congregation which have been assigned as 'portions' to the individual presbyters or shepherds" (*BDAG* 548). Others take it to refer to the plural members of the congregation as "those who are your responsibility to care for" (*LN*

1.464). More likely, it is plural to refer to the different congregations or assemblies over whom the plural "elders" (v. 1) being exhorted exercise oversight, and the "lot" is "the particular congregation entrusted to each of them" (Goppelt 347).[64] Each pastor has a portion of God's larger flock assigned as his responsibility.[65] And no doubt God is the one regarded, though implied, as the assigner.

Positively, the pastor exercises his shepherding influence primarily by being an example to the congregation he leads; note that at this point Peter repeats his identification of the church as "the flock." This is not just the *manner* of his responsibility: there is no "as" in this phrase (as in the negative phrase); the pastor really *is* an example, a *tupos*—again plural because plural elders are addressed. This word means a model, pattern, or example; it can be used for a physical object that serves as a pattern (as in Acts 7:44) or ethically to mean "a model of behavior as an example to be imitated or to be avoided" (*LN* 1.592), here, of course, for emulation. The word is used in Titus 2:7 in a way that illustrates the point well.

Shepherds lead from the front, and the sheep follow; compare John 10:4. Accordingly, the pastor leads by example. To be sure, he instructs the people of God in the ways of God from the Word of God; as discussed in the previous chapter he is, first of all, a teacher. But he models those ways, first, in his own life, or else his influence is ineffective. William Gurnall (2.548) correctly warned, "The minister's practice makes a greater sound than his doctrine. They who forget his sermon, will remember his example" (*CSB*).

---

[64] Selwyn (231) observes that our word *clergy* is derived from *klēroi* ("lots") as it is used here.

[65] This is true even if a plurality of pastors is responsible to exercise watch-care in a single local church.

Consequently, the pastor has no right to exercise dominion over the flock; he is but an under-shepherd assigned his lot in the larger flock of the true Lord of the sheep. "The leaders must oversee the church in a godly way, shepherding the flock rather than domineering it. The pastoral motif of the shepherd caring for and seeking the weak and the wandering . . . provides the background against which these final instructions [of Peter] to the church are to be read" (Jobes 299).

d. A promise to the faithful pastor concludes the words addressed specifically to the elders (literally): "And, the chief shepherd appearing, you will receive the unfading crown of glory" (v. 4).

It is appropriate and encouraging to know that Jesus is the "Chief Shepherd," the Supreme Pastor, if you will. Pastors are under-shepherds, exercising their watch-care under the Lord's own supervision and watch-care. "Peter, addressing presbyter-shepherds, suggests that they are only vicars, that they must carry out their duty in union with Christ, the 'chief of pastors,' in conformity with his instructions and his example" (Spicq 1.208).[66]

Even more encouraging is it to know that He will appear. The Scriptures tell us often that Jesus is coming again. He will make His own appearance in the world and—sobering truth!—He will judge all those to whom He has assigned stewardship responsibilities, including the under-shepherds; compare 1 Corinthians 4:1-5.

Most encouraging of all is to know that the faithful pastor-shepherd will receive the crown. Each word in this promise is interesting. "Receive" is *komizomai*, "to receive as a type of compen-

---

[66] Spicq's discussion of "chief shepherd" (*archipoimēn*) is helpful and provides illustrative material about the use of the word in the N.T. world.

sation" (*LN* 1.572). "Crown" is *stephanos*, not the diadem of a king but the crown of celebration—in Peter's day a wreath or garland placed on a person's head to celebrate victory in the athletic games or in battle or on some other celebratory occasion. "Of glory" is probably a qualitative genitive: thus, "glorious crown," a crown that honors the one who receives it. And "that does not fade away" is *amarantinos*,[67] "not losing the wonderful, pristine character of something—'unfading, not losing brightness, retaining its wonderful character'" (*LN* 1.696).[68] In short, the faithful shepherd-pastor will have a delightful reward.

IMPLICATIONS FOR PRACTICAL APPLICATION

Of the word *shepherd* Hughes (133) says, "This tender, caring, nurturing title suggests a touch here, a kind word there, a gentle prod at the right time. Yet it also suggests resolute strength and protection of the flock." It is obvious that a pastor must have a shepherd's heart.

It would be easy, and dangerous, to read too much into the analogy of a flock of sheep and its shepherd. Sheep, they tell me, are silly, timorous animals, easily straying, easy prey. It is entirely unjustified to suggest that a pastor's people are likewise helpless, often wandering, utterly dependent on the pastor for safety. No Christians should be so impotent and ignorant, and it is in part the pastor's responsibility to see to it that they are strong and capable.

Perhaps the best way to conceive the lessons intended from depicting the church's leaders as shepherds is to rely on some bibli-

---

[67] The English "amaranthine" comes directly from this.

[68] This is the word's only occurrence in the N.T., though a word almost the same occurs in 1 Pet. 1:4, also only there in the N.T.

cal examples of spiritual shepherding. And among the best of these is Jesus' comparison of Himself to a "good shepherd" in John 10. Though I will not attempt to draw out all the helpful truths involved there, some are important enough to mention at least briefly. One of these is the sure knowledge of each other that exists between a shepherd and his sheep. The true shepherd knows his sheep well and calls them, individually, by name (vv. 3, 14). The sheep, in turn, know the voice of their shepherd and follow without hesitation (vv. 3-5). This relationship simply cannot be cultivated in a church apart from the pastor giving focused, individual attention to those for whom he is responsible.

Another truth involved here is that the shepherd leads the sheep and they follow (vv. 3, 4). Only when the pastor leads people aright can he expect them to follow. And only when he leads by example will they even hear his direction. Otherwise, he has no right to their loyalty.

Finally, I must not overlook the point of verse 11: "The good shepherd gives his life for the sheep." It would be possible to read that as applying *only* to Christ, of course. He is certainly the best example of it. But in the context of vv. 10-13, this is a more general principle, contrasting the response of a true shepherd to the behavior of a hireling when the wolf threatens. The shepherd to whom the sheep rightfully belong does not run from danger but loves his sheep and risks his own life for them. So must a faithful pastor love his people enough to sacrifice his own selfish interests, his energies and time, yes and even his life in their behalf.

I leave it to the reader to consider how Psalm 23 might similarly be applied.

CHAPTER 7

THE PASTOR AS LEADER

1 Timothy 3:5: "If a man does not know how to rule his own house, how will he take care of the church of God?"

1 Timothy 5:17: "Let the elders who rule well be counted worthy of double honor."

1 Thessalonians 5:12: "Recognize those who labor among you, and are over you in the Lord and admonish you."

Hebrews 13:7: "Remember those who rule over you, who have spoken the word of God to you: whose faith follow."

Hebrews 13:17: "Obey those who rule over you, and be submissive, for they watch out for your souls."

While all the passages addressed to the pastor speak at least indirectly of his role as a leader, two verbs that are essentially synonyms are especially important in this regard.

1. HEBREWS 13:7, 17, 24 (*hēgeomai*)

The writer of Hebrews thrice refers in the final chapter of his work to "those who rule over you." We may helpfully think of this chapter as an added, epistolary conclusion to the lengthy "sermon" that makes up chapters 1-12. It offers practical instruction to the readers. Indeed, the three verses do not speak directly to the pastor or elders of the church but rather to the church about its attitude toward its leaders. They should "remember" them, follow the example of their faith, and "consider the outcome of their conduct" or way of life (v. 7). They should submissively "obey" them so the leaders can carry out their ministry with joy and not with grief (v. 17). And upon receipt of this letter they should "salute" (KJV) or greet them on behalf of the writer (v. 24).

Although the words are addressed to the church, there is one phrase common to all three verses that speaks to the role and responsibilities of the pastor. That phrase is those who "rule over you": literally "the ones leading you," a plural, substantival participle of *hēgeomai* which means "to so influence others as to cause them to follow a recommended course of action—'to guide, to direct, to lead'" (*LN* 1.465).

This meaning leads naturally into a more official capacity of governing or ruling, as seen in Acts 7:10, which refers to Joseph's role as "governor" over Egypt, or in Luke 3:1 where Pilate is "governor" over Judea. The less official meaning is clearly illustrated in Acts 15:22 where Judas Barsabas and Silas (chosen by the Jerusalem church to accompany Paul and Barnabas back to Antioch with the results of the "Jerusalem Council") are called "*leading men* [KJV, *chief men*] among the brethren." See also Acts 14:12, where Paul is seen as the "*chief* speaker." All of these could be aptly translated as *leaders*.

Whether Hebrews 13 refers to leaders who officially had a governing office is not absolutely certain, but there is no reason to avoid this idea. Though the word *elders* is not used,[69] I am satisfied that these are the ones meant, and that this would at least include the pastors of the congregations receiving the letter. What this word makes clear is that pastors are *leaders* and have official leadership responsibilities to guide the congregation. Though briefly and in passing, the writer of Hebrews mentions some of what the pastor must do in his position as leader.

a. He speaks the Word of God (v. 7). As seen in chapter five, this is the pastor's first duty: to teach the Word of God to his people and so to "feed" the flock.

b. He sets an example in faith (v. 7). That the church should "follow" his faith speaks directly to this responsibility. "Follow" is *mimeomai*, "to behave in the same manner as someone else—'to imitate, to do as others do'" (*LN* 1.509). As seen in chapter six, 1 Peter 5:2, 3 also emphasizes the responsibility of the pastor to lead by example.

In the New Testament *faith* sometimes means *faithfulness*, a meaning that would fit satisfactorily here; but so does the more usual meaning of confidence in God. Perhaps both should be understood, since the one leads immediately into the other. The pastor must be a man of faith, not just saving faith but manifesting a life grounded

---

[69] *Elder(s)* does not appear in Hebrews except in 11:2 where O. T. figures are meant.

on full trust in God. And such a life will necessarily demonstrate faithfulness to his ministry, to the truths of the Christian faith, and to God as manifested in obedience and loyalty. In such a life the pastor sets the example for his flock to imitate.

The other phrase in this verse, "considering the outcome of their conduct," provides the attitude in which imitating the leaders' faith is grounded. Literally, the whole reads, "whose faith be imitating, considering the result of [their] way of life." Many interpreters believe that verse 7 refers to *former* leaders whom the Hebrew Christians could remember, while verses 17 and 24 refer to *present* leaders (Outlaw 360, Kent 281). Whether that is the case does not affect the point of this study. But if that were true the readers could certainly consider the final outcome of the lives of their leaders who had been true to the end. Westcott (434) thinks that those former leaders gave their lives for the faith: "The reference here seems to be to some scene of martyrdom in which the triumph of faith was plainly seen." But Bruce (*Hebrews* 395) is right to insist that all that is needed, here, is that they, like the heroes of chapter 11, died in the faith. Even if verse 7 refers to present leaders, the principle still holds: in Christian living we should always be considering the end result of life, whether yet to come (our own and others we observe) or already witnessed (those who have died). And leaders must set the example in this, demonstrating for all the value of a life of faith and the superior outcome of such a life as compared to a life of unbelieving disobedience of God.

c. He watches for the souls of those he leads (v. 17). "Watch" is *agrupneō*, which literally means to be awake as the opposite of being asleep. While this literal meaning may not appear in the New Testament, Bruce (*Hebrews* 407) suggests that they "lost sleep" over their responsibility; so also Kistemaker (426). Regardless, the word is definitely used of spiritual or mental alertness, of being "awake" or vigilant to needs and dangers that one should be aware of. The idea is very close to that of the watch-care we have seen in the meaning of the word for bishop or overseer.

The pastor, then, exercises such vigilant watch-care, literally, "in behalf of" (*huper*) the souls of those under his shepherding care. The word *soul* (*psuchē*) is used in a variety of ways in the Scriptures: of one's inner *self* or one's *life* or as a synonym for a *person*. In context, here, it appears to refer to the person as a whole, but with some focus on the person as a spiritual being whose eternal welfare is at stake. The NIV translation—"They keep watch over you"—captures the idea of the person correctly but strikes me as too muted.

d. He must give account of his ministry (v. 17). Closely attached to the watch-care of the pastor-shepherd is the observation, literally: "as ones giving back account." The account is given, of course, to God who has placed the pastor in his position of stewardship responsibility to begin with; compare the discussion of the requirement that the pastor be blameless (Tit. 1:7) in chapter three. This sobering truth provides an essential perspective for the pastor's ministry; everything must be done with awareness of finally standing before God to give report and be evaluated by Him who sees everything, including motives, in a perfect light. And he must give account as to how well he has fulfilled the responsibility of exercising watch-care over the souls of those he has led. Serious business indeed! No wonder Augustine (*Sermon* 82.15) said to his congregation, when commenting on this verse, "It is only dread of him that stops me from keeping quiet. I mean to say, who would not much rather keep quiet and not have to give an account of you?" (*ACCS* 10.38).

Jonathan Edwards (77) emphasized this: "There is a time coming when ministers of the Gospel must return to him that sent them, to give him an account of their ministry. As they have been sent forth from him, so they must return again to him. As they have their commission and instructions from him, so they must render an account to him" (*CSB*). Wesley (10.491) made his rhetorical question an emotional one: "And do I know and feel what is implied in 'watching over the souls' of men 'as he that must give account'?" Indeed, one must feel that deeply.

There is some ambiguity about the next clause, literally: "that with joy they may be doing this, and not grieving." What is it that they should be able to do with joy if those in their charge will submit obediently to their leadership? Does the writer mean that they will be able to give account to God with joy? Or does he mean that they can carry out their watch-care responsibilities with joy?

Interpreters differ on this point: Outlaw (372) takes it to mean "give account" with joy; Westcott (445) takes it to mean watch for their souls with joy. Bruce (*Hebrews* 408) apparently thinks of both elements when he says, "The readers are invited to cooperate with their leaders, to make their responsible task easier for them, so that they could discharge it joyfully and not with sorrow," but then compares Phil. 2:16, which refers to Paul's anticipated joy "in the day of Christ."

Though either will be true, I am more inclined to the idea that the believers' submissiveness to the leaders will result in the leaders' being able to carry out their ministry with joy. As Kent (289) observes, the present tense of the participle *do* (*poiōsin*, "be doing"), which looks at the action while it is in progress, seems to be "more appropriate for the leaders' performance of their ministries than of their appearance at the judgment": "If they all respond favorably the work of their leaders becomes increasingly joyful" (Kistemaker 426).

This also seems to fit better with the concluding observation, "for that is unprofitable for you." It is not profitable for the believers to respond to leadership in such a way as to make grievous the work of those who watch for their souls. Indeed, given that the leaders must give account to God, it may even be that the writer is thinking of their report to him about the responsiveness of those under their charge!

2. 1 TIMOTHY 3:4, 5; 5:17; 1 THESSALONIANS 5:12 *(proistamai)*

a. In 1 Timothy 3:4, 5 Paul speaks twice of the pastor as one who must know how to "rule" within his own family. First Timothy 5:17 adds that those who "rule" well should receive "double honor." Romans 12:8 urges those who "rule" to do so with diligence and may be another passing reference to the pastor or elders.[70] In all of these the word is *proistamai*,[71] which literally means to "stand before" and so pictures one who is "up front" as a leader.

---

[70] Some interpreters believe the verb, here, does not mean to lead or rule but to give aid or help to others; it is possible that the immediate context supports that understanding.

[71] Alternately *proistēmi*.

When Paul states the qualification that the pastor must be one who "rules" well his own household (1 Tim. 3:4, 5), he asks how else he will be able to "take care of" God's church. This is an interesting comparison, with "his own" household standing in contrast to "God's" church. And he "rules" his own household while he "takes care of" God's church.

We need to be careful, then, to understand precisely what the verb "rule" (*proistamai*) means. The lexicons list such meanings as *guide, lead, direct, conduct*: "to so influence others as to cause them to follow a recommended course of action" (*LN* 1.465). This glides easily into meanings like "be at the head (of), rule, manage." Interestingly, the word also may have the idea to "show concern for, care for" (*BDAG* 870).[72]

Perhaps all these meanings blend together when referring to the role of the pastor as leader. The word is certainly used, at times, for the pastor's relationship, not just to his family, but to the church. As we have seen, 1 Timothy 5:17 refers to the "elders" that "rule" well. Below, I will deal with 1 Thessalonians 5:12, where Paul appeals to his readers in the church to give respectful recognition to those who labor among them and "are over" them in the Lord. "Are over" is the same verb, in all likelihood viewing the work of the elders in the context.

Even so, it is interesting that in 1 Timothy 3:4, 5, when Paul moves from the pastor's leadership role in his family to the corresponding role in the church, he changes verbs from *proistamai* to

---

[72] *LN* 1:459 renders Tit. 3:8, "'so that those who believe in God may fix their attention on being active in providing help' or '. . . in giving aid.'"

epimeleomai, "take care of," and thus places greater emphasis on the giving of watch-care; Martin (172) appropriately suggests that "the latter term interprets the former." The latter verb means "to care for with diligent concern — 'to care for, to take care of, to provide whatever is needed'" (*LN* 1.463) or "to be concerned about, to give attention so as to respond" (*LN* 1.355). In other literature dating near the time of the New Testament, the verb, with its noun and adverb cognates, was used for the care given to the sick, the care of and devotion to the welfare of children, and ultimately to any task for which one has responsibilities.[73] The fundamental idea of the word suggests that something matters, that it makes a difference to someone. And this leads to the meaning to demonstrate concern, to provide for. As Liefeld (121) notes, the effect of the change from "rule" to "take care of" is that "Paul stresses not authority but the caring side of leadership."

The verb *epimeleomai* ("take care of") appears only twice more in the New Testament, both in Luke 10:34, 35 in the parable of the good Samaritan. This is what the Samaritan did for the man who fell among thieves: he "brought him to an inn and *took care of* him"; and when he left the next day he gave the innkeeper some extra money and said, "*Take care of* him." That steers us in the right direction toward understanding Paul's sense of the work of the pastor.

To be sure, the pastor's ministry to his flock is more than binding up wounds like the good Samaritan, though at times his ministry figuratively includes that! But the breadth of his ministry is encompassed in this good word, *taking care of* the flock. He is its

---

[73] See the helpful article on the word by Spicq (2:47-53).

leader, yes. He has a measure of authority, yes. But he has responsibility even more so, and one that weighs heavily on him.[74] The pastor looks out for the welfare of his flock, which matters to him; he is concerned about them and he manifests that concern in many ways.

b. In 1 Thessalonians 5:12-14 Paul does not use any of the nouns that we have discussed: elder, bishop/overseer, or pastor/shepherd. But he does refer to "those who *are over* you in the Lord," using *proistamai*, the same verb as in 1 Timothy 3 and 5, discussed above. I am satisfied, then, that he is referring to the leaders of the church in terms of their responsibilities, and by any measure the leaders will include the pastor. Indeed, it seems clear to me that what Paul says here refers to the elders of the church: "It seems natural to assume that they were the elders or presbyters of the Thessalonian church" (Hiebert 231).[75] Beale (160) observes: "The idea is of those in an authoritative position of 'managing' or 'shepherding'. . . merely another way of referring to 'elders.'"[76]

As I have said above, the word no doubt has "the primary senses of both 'to lead' and 'to care for'" (*TDNT* 6.702). Bruce (*Thessalonians* 118-19), though he does not think an official sense is involved here in 1 Thessalonians, observes that the word "combines the ideas of leading, protecting and caring for." Knight (232, citing *TDNT*

---

[74] His situation is much like that of Paul in 2 Cor. 11:28, describing (in addition to his external trials in vv. 23-27) the burden that he expressed as "my deep concern for all the churches." The Greek word is different, but the meaning is similar.

[75] Hiebert answers well those who think that these were not ordained officers.

[76] I am aware that some interpreters (Wanamaker 192-95, for example, and others he cites) regard these as persons of some social status who emerged as leaders in providing of their means for the welfare of the Christians, thus serving as patrons or protectors of the church. This involves a "sociological" reading of the letter that does not strike me as adequately grounded in the text. It seems more likely that Paul is referring to elders in this verse, even though he does not use the term.

6.701-02) agrees that the word refers to "one who has been placed before, or at the head of the church, and who has responsibility in that position both to 'rule, lead, or direct' and to 'be concerned for and care for' the church." This is clearly synonymous with the ideas represented by the nouns that identify this office examined in chapter one, especially "bishop/overseer" and "shepherd."

The passage here is addressed to the entire church, identified as "brethren," a form of address used throughout the short letter to the Thessalonians.[77] Specifically, the church is urged to "recognize" (KJV, "know") and "esteem highly" the leaders referred to (vv. 12, 13). To know or recognize them means to count them as the leaders they are, placed in that position both by God's activity and by their own prayerful selection. They must acknowledge their leadership roles and respond with the respect and appreciation that such a role deserves. To esteem them highly means to hold the leaders in highest regard, to count them worthy of the esteem that should be associated with their position. In particular, Paul says this is to be done "in love" and "for their work's sake."

Paul further describes the work assigned to the leaders by two phrases joined closely to "are over you in the Lord." In the original these are three present participles joined under one definite article; it seems clear, then, that the three describe the "work" of one group of persons rather than of three different groups.[78] The group is identified by its function, then, rather than by a title or the name of the office.

---

[77] Fourteen times, in fact: 1:4; 2:1, 9, 14, 17; 3:7; 4:1, 10, 13; 5:1, 4, 12, 14, 25.

[78] This accords with the so-called "Granville-Sharp rule"; though the rule is not 100% true, it is often true and seems clearly to apply here.

The first is that they "labor among you." Labor (*kopiaō*) is a relatively strong word meaning "to engage in hard work, implying difficulties and trouble—'. . . to work hard, to toil, to labor'" (*LN* 1.515). The same verb occurs in 1 Timothy 5:17, treated in chapter five. At the least, the word suggests that the pastor is a leader who expends his strength going about his responsibilities within the flock he shepherds. Paul provides no specific description of the labor involved, but it is clear that this is his way of referring to the work of the pastor, to the various forms of ministering that will be required of him as a leader.

The second is that they "admonish you." This is *noutheteō*, the same word we have examined in Acts 20:31, translated "warn"; see the discussion in chapter six. It indicates serious and systematic instruction and often involves warning about the consequences of wrongdoing or, at times, rebuke and correction when someone has done wrong. "This might be general instruction or, where wrong tendencies had to be corrected, admonition and warning (as in v. 14; 2 Thess. 3:15)" (Bruce, *Thessalonians* 119); "instruction aimed at changing one's moral disposition, with respect to both enlightening and warning the ignorant about potential problems ahead and rebuking those already entangled in wrongdoing" (Beale 161). This will no doubt involve the pastor in personal interaction with members of his flock, though it will be grounded in the public ministry of teaching the Word.

This picture of the duties of the pastor-leader is well balanced. Though the wording is broad and general, rather than specific or illustrative, it makes a strong impression. The pastor (with other leaders, no doubt) works diligently among those under his charge, ministering to them in various ways. He is their leader "in the Lord," providing them guidance and watch-care. He instructs them in the Word of God, urging them in how they should walk and warning them how they should not, even correcting them when they have strayed.

And the congregation should respond with recognition, love, and high esteem. As implied by the command at the end of verse 13, when the leaders give good direction and the people follow with respect, there will be peace within the fellowship. Bruce (*Thessalonians* 120) observes, helpfully:

> It will make for the effective life and witness of the church and for peaceful relations among its members if its leaders are recognized and honored and their directions followed. The corollary of this is that the leaders should be the kind of people who deserve to be recognized and honored by their fellow Christians . . . . Such leaders did not do the appropriate work because they had been appointed as leaders; they were recognized as leaders because they were seen to be doing the work.

Bruce (*Thessalonians* 122) also discusses the view of Chrysostom and others that verse 14 is addressed to the leaders rather than to the congregation in general.[79] He disagrees and observes that the wording is exactly parallel to verse 12 and that it is "natural" to suppose that the same "brethren" are meant in both places, adding: "The various forms of service enjoined

---

[79] For Chrysostom's view, see his homily on 1 Thess. 5:12, 14 (*NPNF1* 13.367).

in the words that follow are certainly a special responsibility of leaders, but not their exclusive responsibility: they are ways in which all the members of the community can fulfill the direction of verse 11 to encourage and strengthen one another."

I think Bruce is right: verse 14 is addressed to the whole church. Even so, the verse deserves some attention, since *it indicates the mutual responsibilities and relationships, within the congregation, which the pastor must take the lead in and work to foster within the church.* Four such matters are named, to be mentioned here only briefly.

1. "Warn those who are unruly." "Warn" is the same word (*noutheteō*) translated "admonish" in verse 12 (see above); the instruction includes working to correct those who are in error: namely, the "unruly." This word, *ataktos*, means being out of order, disorderly. It was sometimes used in a military context for those who broke ranks; these are out of step with the church in their behavior and attitudes. They need others in the church to warn them of the error of their ways and work to bring them back in line. And though this is not the work of the pastor alone, surely he must set an example in this regard and teach the church how to exercise this discipline.[80]

2. "Comfort the faint-hearted (KJV, feebleminded)." This is *oligopsuchos*, which literally means "little-souled." In other words,

---

[80] In the context of the entire letter to the Thessalonians, the "unruly" may well be the same as those who are referred to in 4:11, 12; see also 2 Thess. 3:6-13, where "disorderly" (vv. 6, 11) has the same root. These we sometimes call "idlers"; they were apparently not working for their own upkeep and creating a burden on the church for their support. But Paul's words will apply broadly to those who are disorderly and create disorder of any kind—unless there is outright immorality that makes clear that the offenders are not Christians (as in 1 Cor. 5).

these are those who are discouraged and in danger of giving up the Christian journey: "those whose spirit is all but broken" (Ward 115). "Comfort" is *paramutheomai*, "to console, to comfort, to encourage" (*LN* 1.306). When some in the church are losing heart, others must encourage them and help them gain back their determination to press on. And the pastor leads in this and fosters the kind of mutual concern for one another that leads believers to respond quickly in such a fashion.

3. "Uphold the weak." The weak are those who are sick; *astheneō* apparently refers, here, to spiritual infirmity: "any who find that they are weak when assailed by hardship or temptation" (Marshall 151). The verb *support* is *antechomai*, which literally suggests the idea of holding oneself against someone in order to help them stand; thus it means to help or, in this context, to assist or strengthen. When a believer suffers some illness of soul, another needs to come to the rescue, to stand with him until he can stand on his own. And the pastor, exemplifying this in his own ministry, needs to cultivate such a caring responsiveness within his congregation.

4. "Be patient with all." There is a question, here, whether "all" means all in the church or all people in general, including the lost. Most certainly we should be patient toward everyone in the world, but in context it is more likely that "all" refers to all within the Christian community, broadened now from the three specific groups just referred to. "Be patient" is *makrothumeō*, which literally pictures keeping passion at a distance: "a state of emotional calm in the face of provocation or misfortune and without complaint or irritation" (*LN* 1.307). Thus it means to be slow to anger, patient in dealing

with others regardless how they behave or act toward us, and especially when they have mistreated us. In Ephesians 4:2 the same word is translated "longsuffering" and further explained as "bearing with one another in love."

No doubt responding to the first three of these four appeals will require the patience of the fourth. But so will countless other situations within the life of the church, all of them demanding mutual watch-care for one another. Again, then, the pastor leads by exemplifying this kind of patience and nurtures this kind of loving action within the entire congregation.

These four provide excellent examples of the shepherding watch-care required of the pastor in particular and of the church members in general. The observations of Holmes (186) along this line are well made:

> With respect to 5:14, it is important to notice that Paul calls on the entire congregation, not just the leaders, to take responsibility for mutual care and encouragement (cf. 5:11 above). As Ernest Best (233) observes, "Paul lays the responsibility for the whole community on the community itself; each member, and not the leaders alone, must be aware of his or her responsibility for others and seek to help them." . . . In short, Paul is trying to develop in the entire congregation a sense of pastoral responsibility.

IMPLICATIONS FOR PRACTICAL APPLICATION

So what sort of *leader* is a pastor? He *is* a leader, of course. Like all leaders he has responsibilities for others' actions and must therefore have a level of authority that is commensurate with those responsibilities. Kistemaker (426) is right to say, "The appeal to obey them and to submit to their authority is timely . . . . If a leader is a dedicated minister of the Word of God, he proves thereby that Christ has given him authority. And if Christ has entrusted him with the task of assuming leadership, the people need not question his authority."

Even so, the picture drawn in this chapter—and indeed in this entire work—is one that tempers the exercise of that authority with an overriding concern for the spiritual welfare of his congregation. He *governs*, to be sure. But he governs primarily by teaching believers how to apply the Word of God in their lives. He leads by setting the example before them. He leads by exercising watch-care for their spiritual well-being. He leads by fostering within the congregation an active, mutual watch-care for one another.

In short, the pastor is a *servant-leader*. He first demonstrates the principle defined by Jesus that those who would be great must be great in serving. I find it interesting and compelling that Luke 22:25, 26 uses the same word for leading—*hēgeomai*—that is used three times in Hebrews 13, as discussed above. Of such a leader Jesus says that he must be as one *serving*. Of course this is easier to say than to practice, as Snodgrass (214) observes: "Though Christians talk about servant leadership, it rarely exists." He goes on to say that pastors do not really believe in servant leadership, one reason being that all of us find it difficult to separate leadership from the "exercise of the ego." He concludes: "The servant leadership Jesus requires is only that application of the gospel to the task of leadership. If leaders cannot apply the gospel to themselves, they are not leaders."

I once heard (via tape recording) a well-known pastor, in a conference for other pastors, talking about his strong belief in the authority of pastoral leadership. He illustrated by saying that if he were to return to his church and announce that the Lord had told him that his church should become Roman Catholic, the chairman of the deacon board should arise and say, "Yes, Father, how soon can we join them?" That pastor should be ashamed, and not merely because of his unilateral leadership style. He should be ashamed primarily because he had not taught his people to think for themselves, to know the principles of the Scripture well enough to recognize even a leader's error! As Luther (39.307) observed, the principle in John 10:5, 8, 27 means that "it is the sheep who are to judge whether they[81] teach the voice of Christ or the voice of strangers," judging on the basis of the Word of God, which is the possession of all the church.

I have said already, but I will repeat here at the closing of this chapter: in any management position, a leader who has to depend on exerting his authority to get his way will ultimately fail, usually sooner than later. In the church, especially, a pastor with a shepherd's heart is a servant-leader. He wins not by intimidation but by persuasion. He leads by example. He gains his people's respect not so much by asserting it as by demonstrating his genuine concern for them. As Forlines (4/80) puts it, "Ministerial authority is exercised by preaching, teaching, rebuking, exhorting, admonishing and such like." He influences God's flock by teaching them the Word of God and how to apply it to their lives. Likewise Stewart (213): "Whence comes this authority? It springs, first, from the fact that it is God's Word, not our own, that we proclaim."

---

[81] Luther's "they" are "bishops, pope, scholars, and everyone else" who teaches.

AFTERWORD: MOVING FORWARD

The biblical picture of the pastor and his work, drawn in the preceding chapters, is sobering. For that matter, it may be intimidating. Even so, we must not back away from the challenge; we must set our course in light of the biblical teaching and move in that direction.

WHAT THE PASSAGES DO NOT SAY

Though the biblical picture may be challenging, it is not complete. As I analyzed the passages individually and then thought about them as a whole, I became acutely aware that some important things were not being said. For example, the passages do not say that a pastor must be filled with the Spirit of God, which Lloyd-Jones (109) calls "the first and the greatest qualification." Perhaps the reason is that this is obvious, or that it is said about all believers (Eph. 5:18). Certainly a pastor must be Spirit-filled; Acts 6:3 assumes as much in requiring that even the seven chosen to supervise the "daily ministration" to widows must be "full of the Holy Ghost." How much more the shepherd of the flock! All ministry that glorifies God and is effective must be done in the fullness and power of the Holy Spirit.

Nor do any of the passages prescribe that a pastor must be a man of prayer. Again, this is an obvious requirement, apparently reflected in Acts 6:4 when the apostles insisted that they would "give [themselves] continually to prayer, and to the ministry of the word." To be sure, all Christians must be people of prayer and the pastor must set the example. Prayer is—among other things—the expression of one's need for God, a sign of dependence on Him for direction and effectiveness.

Furthermore, the passages do not tell us that a pastor must be an active witness for Christ, working to win people to faith. Perhaps the reason for this is that the passages focus—properly so—on the man's relationship to the church. But the requirement that one must "have a good testimony among those who are outside" (1 Tim. 3:7) turns attention to the pastor's relationship to sinners. One reason underlying this requirement is that his witness to them will be fruitless unless he has their confidence. A spiritually healthy church is one where the unsaved are being influenced for Christ, and the pastor must set the tone and the agenda for outreach.

I also noticed that nothing is said about the pastor's education. This is not surprising, given the great difference between their circumstances and ours. In the days of the apostles and their letters to the early churches there were no Christian colleges or seminaries to prepare potential pastors for the ministry. Even so, I do not doubt that the apostles insisted that candidates give themselves to earnest, careful, and continuing study of the Word of God, and perhaps of other resources for improvement in their ministry. In our day, by contrast, means of education are close at hand and relatively easy to access. For most, a comprehensive, formal preparation for the ministry can be completed in just a few years dedicated to that objective.[82] Beyond this, there is the opportunity to serve as an apprentice under the tutelage of an experienced pastor. I am more certain than ever that a "call" to the ministry is by definition a call to prepare, and the better prepared one is the more effective he can expect to be. Would-be pastors need a Bible-centered, character-building education!

---

[82] Which does not mean, of course, that one's "education" is finished when formal degrees are obtained!

But it goes beyond my purpose to expand further on the things that the passages treated do *not* say; in addition to these four there are many others I could mention. My purpose, instead, has been to focus on the things these passages say about the pastor and his role. My hope is that all pastors and potential pastors will clearly understand what the New Testament has to say about their character and work.

In fact, although the passages do not say everything, they say a great deal, so much that the pastor-to-be (not to mention the pastor-already) may find himself wondering just how to measure up, how to be everything a shepherd of the flock of God ought to be. Indeed, our churches require many things of those who exercise spiritual watch-care over them and give them leadership. The pastorate is noble and demanding.

SOME PRACTICAL SUGGESTIONS

There are, of course, no shortcuts. I cannot possibly provide the reader with a few suggestions that guarantee success. As I indicated in the Foreword, my purpose in this book is not to tell anyone how to preach or how to be a pastor. Even now, I do not mean to stray far from the clear implications of exegesis. I will therefore only make some concluding observations, aimed directly at the reader, about how the pastor can aim toward being the man described in the passages chosen for exegesis in this book. While these observations should be useful for any pastor at any stage of his ministry, they are especially important for the man who is making preparation for ordination. Do you sense that God is calling, or has called, you to a pastoral ministry? Here, among numerous others that might be mentioned, are seven strong recommendations. They are but briefly described; I recommend that you define each one in greater detail.

1. Become a man of prayer.

As I've said, prayer is needing God, depending on Him, seeking His face, direction, and help. You need to pray earnestly about many things, and some fasting in connection with prayer may well help ensure your own intensity therein. Pray fervently about your sense of calling; make sure God wants you in the ministry. Pray for the fullness and unction of the Spirit in your life, your preaching, and your interactions with others in and out of the church. Pray for God's leadership in what you do and how you do it, sincerely submitting to that leadership. Pray for the effectiveness that comes only when you seek for Him to work through you and get the glory to Himself. In addition, pray for those whom you lead, as a church *and individually.* The shepherd ministers to the sheep.

Stewart (202) cites Chalmers as saying that most failures in the ministry are due to lack of prayer. You simply *must* have a regular and meaningful devotional life. Your time with God sets the tone for the life of the church and your servant leadership.

2. Give yourself to a lifetime of careful study of the Scriptures.

Perhaps I have said enough about the fact that your primary responsibility within the flock is to teach them the Word of God for their doctrine and life. Absolutely essential to carrying out this responsibility is that you be a faithful student of what He has revealed of Himself and His will. You need daily study of the Bible both for yourself and for your program of preaching and teaching. Your study needs to be systematic and comprehensive, digging for what the text really says and for what it means in Christian practice. Forlines (11/80) is right to observe that people will continue to listen attentively only to a pastor who is "growing in his knowledge of the Bible and its application to life."

Understand, now, that you must grapple with the Scriptures devotionally and personally, and not just for sermon material! I commend the words of James S. Stewart (108) on this point:

> Let there be a deeper constraint behind your Bible study than the feverish question, "Now what am I going to preach about next Sunday?" If all our people need the devotional use of the Bible for their spiritual nourishment and growth in grace, how much more do we . . . ! Nothing can atone for slackness and indiscipline at this point. Let us give ourselves day by day to prayerful and meditative study of the Word, listening to hear what God the Lord will speak: lest, when we seek to interpret the Scriptures to others, it should have to be said of us, in the words of the Samaritan . . .
> "Thou hast nothing to draw with, and the well is deep!"

Nor should this lifetime study be limited to the biblical text, even though that is the primary thing. You ought to give careful attention to a broad program of reading, including especially works complementary to biblical study like theology, church history, and the sermons of great preachers.[83]

---

[83] Lloyd-Jones' recommended program of reading for preachers (171-183) is insightful.

Here then is something else to pray about: namely, for spiritual enlightenment and understanding of the Word. Divine illumination is essential. But prayer is no substitute for the hard work of skilled exegesis and practical application.

3. Develop your ability to prepare and deliver sermons.

The pastor's pulpit ministry is the foundation for everything else. If God wants you to be a pastor, you can preach effectively. Your natural talent, however, will not be enough to guarantee that. You need to continue, throughout your lifetime, to improve. Learn all you can about good homiletic skills. Read the sermons of the masters. Write out key passages of your sermons, adding a touch of eloquence here and there. Work on your delivery: record some of your sermons and listen to them for your own critique, and get someone else who will be honest with you to listen and comment. Preaching is like any other skill: practice makes perfect only if you learn from your mistakes and strive to get better.

Again, pray. Pray for God's help in this and, even more important, for His anointing on your preaching.

4. Practice self discipline.

This is one of the Christian graces, at the heart of many of the practical qualifications dealt with in chapters three and four. Among the negative qualities defined were not being addicted to alcoholic beverages or drugs, not being greedy for shameful gain or covetous, not being quick-tempered or quarrelsome. Among the positive qualities were being sober-minded and self-controlled and completely faithful to one's wife. The key to all such qualities is self-discipline.

In essence, self-discipline means that one's better judgment prevails over lesser inclinations. It happens when you make yourself do what you know you ought to do even when you feel inclined to do otherwise. The better self, in submission to God's will, becomes the master. You study, or pray, or make visits, or prepare sermons when you ought to, rather than allowing other interests to divert you. You even play when it's right for you to play, or for that matter bathe and brush your teeth when you ought to. Self-discipline practiced in any area, for that matter, can help in other areas.

There is probably no vocation where a man may give in to laziness, without being held accountable, so much as that of a pastor. As Stewart (195) says, "Slackness is such an insidious peril." There is no clock to punch and no "boss" to set your schedule. *Self*-discipline is therefore required. And, by the way, being constantly busy, "on the go," is not necessarily a sign of fruitful labor; again, self-discipline is required.

So pray. Self discipline is, after all, part of "the fruit of the Spirit" (Gal. 9:23; KJV, *temperance*) and you can have God's help in developing this quality. Even so, *you* must exercise your will, and that will make the difference whether you are master or slave of your inclinations and desires.

5. Guard your character.

If the qualifications of a pastor studied in chapters three and four mean anything at all, they mean that a pastor must be a man of character, practicing integrity within and in all his dealings with others. Most downfalls are traceable to failures here. Make a settled commitment to be upright in all you do.

But more than a once-for-all commitment is needed: you have to adopt practices that work to safeguard your character commitments, both in your own eyes and in the eyes of others, not to mention the Great Pastor of all the church. In 2 Corinthians 8:18-21 Paul records that an unnamed brother was chosen to travel with him and his associates in raising funds to take to Jerusalem; the purpose was to avoid any reason for blame and so to provide things honest not only in the sight of the Lord but also in the sight of the people involved. This served both to protect Paul from temptation and to keep his reputation unassailable.

Depending on your circumstances, there are many such things you should consider doing for the sake of both your character (what you really are) and your reputation (what others think you are). Watch your counseling practices! There are circumstances when you should have someone else with you, like when you are handling the church's funds or visiting a woman who is alone. I recommend that you involve someone whom you trust and make yourself accountable to that person, especially in matters where temptation is strong. Perhaps someone should ask you what you watched when you were away, alone, in a hotel room. I know of one pastor who would not travel unless his wife could accompany him.

Once more, pray. Pray for God Himself to make and keep you clean, to guard your character. And while you're at it, ask Him to help you have the wisdom to adopt practices that encourage integrity.

6. Give your family the attention they deserve.

The list of qualifications in both 1 Timothy and Titus (see chapter three) makes it impossible to miss the importance of this. The shepherd of the church must first be the shepherd of his own family. They need your time and energies; lead and develop them and learn from that how to lead and develop others.

Many a man of God has lost his own family by neglect and blamed his dedication to ministry. Your wife and children are also part of the flock of God for whom He has given you watch-care responsibility. If you minister to others and not to them you will have failed as a husband, as a father, and as a pastor. In your own family you must set the example for all the other families in the church.

Do you pray for your wife and children?

7. Work on your people skills.

This final suggestion reflects the fact that the pastor's concern is ultimately with people. He must please God, of course, and will be judged on the basis of his faithfulness to God's calling. But he can be faithful to that calling only to the degree that he leads, shapes, and influences people.

The pastor's role as a teacher is subject to the old saying that a teacher hasn't taught if his students haven't learned. It may be true that this is not an absolute, that students sometimes resist good teaching. But in the end the fruit of a pastor's labors is found in the lives of the people to whom he ministers. Whatever else may be said, a pastor's work is with people, both within and without the church.

Consequently, the effective pastor needs to be able to work well with people, and this includes working with them as individuals and families; not just from behind the podium when preaching or presiding over a church business meeting, but in their homes and in the marketplace.

It would be easy to misunderstand me. I am not referring to what some people call "social skills" or to what others call a "charismatic" personality. Some of us are charming and some of us are not. But regardless of one's natural personality, a pastor can learn how to work well with others, how to be winsome and gracious, positive and persuasive in public and in private, without being artificial. The positive qualities discussed in chapter three make important contributions to this.

The effective pastor must therefore get out among his people, get to know them and their needs and to be known by them as a real person. That is the foundation for ministering to them, and that includes praying with and for them.

No one ever said that being a faithful, effective pastor is easy. The demands are many and weighty. But the ministry is the Lord's and His reward is the one that matters. Paul's attitude in this is a good example for any pastor:

> Let a man so consider us, as servants of Christ and stewards of the mysteries of God. Moreover it is required in stewards that one be found faithful. . . . Therefore judge nothing before the time, until the Lord comes, who will both bring to light the hidden things of darkness and reveal the counsels of the hearts; and then each one's praise will come from God (1 Cor. 4:1, 2, 5).

BIBLIOGRAPHY

Reference Works (cited according to these abbreviations)

ACCS—Ancient Christian Commentary on Scripture: New Testament, ed. Peter Gorday, gen. ed. Thomas C. Oden (Downers Grove, IL: InterVarsity, 2000).

AF—The Apostolic Fathers, ed. Kirsopp Lake (2 vols.; Loeb Classical Library; Cambridge, Massachusetts: Harvard University Press, 1912; 1959 reprint).

BDAG—A Greek-English Lexicon of the New Testament and Other Early Christian Literature, 3rd edition, rev. and ed. by Frederick William Danker, based on Walter Bauer's German lexicon, sixth edition, and on previous English editions by Arndt, Gingrich, and Danker (Chicago: University of Chicago Press, 2000).

CSB—Classic Study Bible, accessed at http://armsdev.realtracs.net/ beng/ and quoted with permission from its editor, Paul V. Harrison. (In most instances I have provided the original source of the quotation as indicated by the editor.)

LN—Greek-English Lexicon of the New Testament Based on Semantic Domains, second ed., ed. J. P. Louw and E. A. Nida (2 vols; New York: United Bible Societies, 1988, 1989).

NPNF1—Nicene and Post-Nicene Fathers, 1st Series, ed. Philip Schaff (14 vols.; Grand Rapids: Eerdmans, 1956).

NPNF2—Nicene and Post-Nicene Fathers, 2d Series, ed. Philip Schaff and Henry Wace (14 vols.; Grand Rapids:Eerdmans, 1956).

TDNT—Theological Dictionary of the New Testament, ed. Gerhard Kittel, trans. Geoffrey W. Bromiley (10 vols.; Grand Rapids: Eerdmans, 1964).

Other Works (cited by author's last name)

Baxter, Richard, *The Reformed Pastor*, abridged and edited by James M. Houston (Portland, Oregon: Multnomah, 1982).

Beale, G. K., *1-2 Thessalonians* (IVPNTC; Downers Grove, IL: InterVarsity, 2003).

Best, Ernest, *A Commentary on the First and Second Epistles to the Thessalonians* (HNTC; New York: Harper & Row, 1972; reprint, Peabody, Mass.: Hendrickson, 1987).

Boice, James Montgomery, *Acts: An Expositional Commentary* (Grand Rapids: Baker, 1997).

Bruce, F. F., *Commentary on the Epistle to the Hebrews* (NICNT; Grand Rapids: Eerdmans, 1964).

Bruce, F. F., *Word Biblical Commentary: 1 & 2 Thessalonians* (Waco, TX: Word Books, 1982).

Calvin, John, *Calvin's Commentaries* (22 vols.; Grand Rapids: Baker, 1998).

Chrysostom, John: *Nicene and Post-Nicene Fathers,* 1st Series (see reference works, above).

Edwards, Jonathan, *The Salvation of Souls: Nine Previously Unpublished Sermons on the Call to Ministry and the Gospel,* ed. Richard A. Bailey and Gregory A. Wills (Wheaton, Ill.: Crossway, 2002).

Fee, Gordon D., *1 and 2 Timothy, Titus* (NIBC; Peabody, Mass.: Hendrickson, 1984, 1988).

Forlines, Leroy, "The Pastor and His People" in sixteen parts (January 1980 to April 1981) in *Contact* (published monthly by the Executive Office of the National Association of Free Will Baptists). Quotations are referenced by month and year.

Gealy, F. D., *The First and Second Epistles to Timothy and the Epistle to Titus* (IB, vol. 11; Nashville: Abingdon, 1955).

Goppelt, Leonhard, *A Commentary on I Peter,* trans. John E. Alsup (Grand Rapids: Eerdmans, 1993).

Gurnall, William: *The Christian in Complete Armour: a Treatise of the Saints' War Against the Devil* (2 vols. in one; Edinburgh: Banner of Truth Trust, 1964 reprint).

Hiebert, D. Edmond, *The Thessalonian Epistles* (Chicago: Moody Press, 1971).

Hillyer, Norman, *1 and 2 Peter, Jude* (NIBC; Peabody, Mass.: Hendrickson, 1992).

Hoehner, Harold W., *Ephesians: An Exegetical Commentary* (Grand Rapids: Baker, 2002).

Holmes, Michael W., *The NIV Application Commentary: 1 & 2 Thessalonians* (Grand Rapids: Zondervan, 1998).

Hughes, R. Kent, *Preaching the Word: Ephesians* (Wheaton: Crossway, 1990) (Used by permission of Crossway books, www.crossway.com).

Jobes, Karen H., *1 Peter* (BECNT; Grand Rapids: Baker, 2005).

Kelly, J. N. D., *A Commentary on the Pastoral Epistles* (HNTC; New York: Harper & Row, 1964).

Kent, Homer A., Jr., *The Pastoral Epistles* (Chicago: Moody Press, 1982 rev.).

Kistemaker, Simon J., *New Testament Commentary: Exposition of the Epistle to the Hebrews* (Grand Rapids: Baker, 1984).

Knight, George W., III, *The Pastoral Epistles* (NIGTC; Grand Rapids: Eerdmans, 1992).

Larkin, William J., Jr., *Acts* (IVPNTC; Downers Grove, Ill.: InterVarsity, 1995).

Lea, Thomas D., "1, 2 Timothy" in *The New American Commentary: 1, 2 Timothy, Titus* (Nashville: Broadman, 1992) (Reprintd and used by permission).

Lenski, R. C. H., *The Interpretation of St. Paul's Epistles to the Colossians, to the Thessalonians, to Timothy, to Titus and to Philemon* (Columbus, Ohio: Wartburg, 1946).

Liefeld, Walter L., *The NIV Application Commentary: 1 and 2 Timothy, Titus* (Grand Rapids: Zondervan, 1999).

Lloyd-Jones, D. Martyn, *Preaching and Preachers* (Grand Rapids: Zondervan, 1971).

Luther, Martin, *Luther's Works,* ed. Jaroslav Pelikan (55 vols.; St. Louis: Concordia Publishing, 1957).

Marshall, I. Howard, *A Critical and Exegetical Commentary on the Pastoral Epistles* (ICC; Edinburgh: T & T Clark, 1999).

Martin, D. Michael, *The New American Commentary: 1, 2 Thessalonians* (Nashville: Broadman and Holman, 1995) (Reprintd and used by permission).

Mounce, William D., *Word Biblical Commentary: Pastoral Epistles* (Nashville: Thomas Nelson, 2000).

Nazianzen, Gregory, *Nicene and Post-Nicene Fathers,* 2nd Series (see reference works, above).

O'Brien, Peter T., *The Letter to the Ephesians* (PNTC; Grand Rapids: Eerdmans, 1999).

Outlaw, Stanley, *The Randall House Bible Commentary: The Book of Hebrews* (Nashville: Randall House, 2005).

Packer, J. I., *A Passion for Faithfulness: Wisdom From the Book of Nehemiah* (Wheaton: Crossway, 1995) (Used by permission of Crossway books, www.crossway.com).

Schnackenburg, Rudolf, *The Epistle to the Ephesians,* trans. Helen Heron (Edinburgh: T&T Clark, 1991).

Selwyn, E. G., *The First Epistle of St. Peter* (London: Macmillan, 1958) (Reproduced with permission of Palgrave Macmillan).

Snodgrass, Klyne, *The NIV Application Commentary: Ephesians* (Grand Rapids: Zondervan, 1996).

Spicq, Ceslas, *Theological Lexicon of the New Testament* (3 vols; Peabody, Mass: Hendrickson, 1994).

Spurgeon, Charles, *Spurgeon's Lectures to His Students,* condensed and abridged by David Otis Fuller and William Culbertson, 3rd ed. (Grand Rapids: Zondervan, 1945).

Stewart, James S., *Heralds of God* (New York: Charles Scribner's Sons, 1956).

Stott, John R. W., *Guard the Truth: The Message of 1 Timothy & Titus* (Downers Grove, Ill.: InterVarsity, 1996).

Stott, John R. W., *The Spirit, the Church and the World: The Message of Acts* (Downers Grove, Ill.: InterVarsity, 1990).

Thielicke, Helmut, *The Ethics of Sex,* trans. John W. Doberstein (New York: Harper & Row, 1964).

Wanamaker, Charles A., *The Epistles to the Thessalonians* (NIGTC; Grand Rapids: Eerdmans, 1990).

Ward, Ronald A., *Commentary on 1 & 2 Thessalonians* (Waco, TX: Word Books, 1973).

Wesley, John, *The Works of John Wesley* (14 vols.; Grand Rapids: Zondervan, n.d.: reproduced from the 1872 edition).

Westcott, B. F., *The Epistle to the Hebrews* (Grand Rapids: Eerdmans, 1955).

White, Newport J. D., "The First and Second Epistles to Timothy and the Epistle to Titus," *The Expositor's Greek Testament,* ed. W. Robertson Nicoll (five vols; Grand Rapids: Eerdmans, 1951),

Williams, David J., *New International Biblical Commentary: Acts* (Peabody, Mass.: Hendrickson, 1985, 1990).

THE WORKS OF
JAMES ARMINIUS

Introduction by Stephen M. Ashby
$179.99
ISBN 0892655674

This 3 volume set of the writings of James Arminius
is a classic collection of benchmark constructive
theology. Scholars interested in the Calvinist-
Arminian debate as well as students of the history of
Christian thought will find this collection thought-
provoking as well as helpful.

To order call **1-800-877-7030** or
visit our website at **www.RandallHouse.com**

THE RANDALL HOUSE
COMMENTARY SERIES

The *Randall House Bible Commentary* series is a must have for pastors and students alike. With Robert Picirilli as General Editor and all Free Will Baptist contributors, the *Randall House Bible Commentary* series is a great addition to any library.

$29.99 Each or All 8 for Only $199.99!

Mark   *Picirilli*
ISBN 0892655003

John   *Stallings*
ISBN 0892651377

1 and 2 Corinthians   *Picirilli*
ISBN 0892659491

Galatians-Colossians   *Marberry, Ellis, Picirilli*
ISBN 0892651342

1 Thessalonians- Philemon *Ellis, Outlaw, Picirilli*
ISBN 0892651431

Hebrews   *Outlaw*
ISBN 0892655143

James, 1 and 2 Peter, Jude *Harrison, Picirilli*
ISBN 0892651458

To order call **1-800-877-7030** or
visit our website at **www.RandallHouse.com**

Simple:
The Christian Life Doesn't Have to Be Complicated

Robert J. Morgan

$7.99 or $4.99 each when purchased in quantities of 24
ISBN 0892655623

The ideal book for church guests and new believers, *Simple* walks
the reader through the ABC's of the Christian faith.

To order call **1-800-877-7030** or
visit our website at **www.RandallHouse.com**

LEADING FROM YOUR STRENGTHS:
Team-Building Discovery Kit

Dr. John Trent and Rodney Cox

$249.99
ISBN 0892655216

The *Leading From Your Strengths Team-Building Discovery Kit* is designed to help you and your team better understand your unique strengths and how to blend and build those strengths in a way that helps you be more productive, efficient, and creative than ever before.

To order call **1-800-877-7030** or
visit our website at **www.RandallHouse.com**

Regaining Balance:
91 Days of Prayer and Praise

Randy Sawyer

$9.99 or $7.49 each when purchased
in quantities of 25 or more
ISBN 0892655186

Regaining Balance is a devotional journal designed to guide its readers through a season of spiritual revival. Each day of the 91-day journal encourages involvement in a handful of spiritual disciplines in order to help the reader regain focus and balance in every aspect of life.

To order call **1-800-877-7030** or
visit our website at **www.RandallHouse.com**

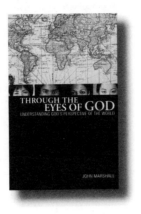

THROUGH THE EYES OF GOD

John Marshall

$9.99
ISBN 0892655135

After spending years in the pastorate, John Marshall realized that he was nothing more than a spectator in his involvement in the Great Commission. This recognition sparked questions and a curiosity—What does God really say about missions? Out of these concerns came a God-ordained journey for him and his church that has changed lives, impacted thousands, and made an eternal difference.

To order call **1-800-877-7030** or
visit our website at **www.RandallHouse.com**

UNDERSTANDING ASSURANCE and SALVATION

Robert E. Picirilli

$6.99
ISBN 0892656360

Through a basic overview of the teachings of Joseph Arminius, Picirilli discusses the biblical explanation of the possibility of apostasy. This booklet presents the Reformed Arminian position of assurance and salvation in easy-to-understand terms that prove beneficial to both scholar and layperson.

To order call **1-800-877-7030** or
visit our website at **www.RandallHouse.com**